John Telford

The popular history of Methodism

John Telford

The popular history of Methodism

ISBN/EAN: 9783742843579

Manufactured in Europe, USA, Canada, Australia, Japa

Cover: Foto ©ninafisch / pixelio.de

Manufactured and distributed by brebook publishing software
(www.brebook.com)

John Telford

The popular history of Methodism

THE

POPULAR HISTORY

OF

❦ METHODISM. ❦

BY

JOHN TELFORD, B.A.

London:

CHARLES H. KELLY, 2, CASTLE STREET, CITY ROAD, E.C.;
AND 66, PATERNOSTER ROW, E.C.

1896

THE

POPULAR HISTORY

OF

❧ METHODISM. ❧

BY

JOHN TELFORD, B.A.

London:

CHARLES H. KELLY, 2, CASTLE STREET, CITY ROAD, E.C.;
AND 66, PATERNOSTER ROW, E.C.

1896

CONTENTS.
CHAPTER I.
PREPARATION FOR METHODISM.

CHAPTER II.
THE EVANGELIST OF ENGLAND.

CHAPTER III.
METHODISM SINCE WESLEY'S DEATH.

HISTORY AND POLITY OF METHODISM

The History of Wesleyan Methodism, from its Origin to the Conference of 1849. By Dr. George Smith. Three vols., post 8vo, 15s.

Stevens, Abel, LL.D. THE HISTORY OF METHODISM, from its Origin to the Centenary. Three Volumes. Crown 8vo, 10s. 6d.

American Methodism, A Compendious History of. By Abel Stevens, LL.D. Crown 8vo, 550 pp., with Portraits, 5s.

A Handbook of Scriptural Church Principles, and of Wesleyan Methodist History and Polity. By the Rev. Benjamin Gregory, D.D. Crown 8vo, with Index, 3s. 6d.

Rigg, Rev. J. H., D.D. THE CHURCHMANSHIP OF JOHN WESLEY, and the Relations of Wesleyan Methodism to the Church of England. New and Revised Edition. Crown 8vo, 2s. 6d.
—— THE CONNEXIONAL ECONOMY OF WESLEYAN METHODISM, in its Ecclesiastical and Spiritual Aspects. Crown 8vo, 3s. 6d.

John Wesley, The Church of England and Wesleyan Methodism: Their Relation to each other clearly and fully explained in Two Dialogues. 1.—Was John Wesley a High Churchman? 2.—Is Modern Methodism Wesleyan Methodism? Crown 8vo, cloth, 1s.

Methodism in the Light of the Early Church. By the Rev. W. F. Slater, M.A. Paper covers, 1s. 6d.; cloth, 2s. 6d.

Methodism: A Parallel. By W. A. Quick, of the Victoria Conference, Australia. 8vo, 3s. 6d.

Methodism, The Mission of. By the Rev. Richard Green. Fernley Lecture of 1890. Paper covers, 2s., cloth, 3s.

The Prose Works of the Rev. John Wesley. Library Edition. 14 vols., demy 8vo, 49s.

Fifty-three Sermons of Rev. John Wesley. Crown 8vo, 3s. 6d.
These Sermons, with the Notes on the New Testament, constitute the Standard Doctrines of the Methodist Connexion.

Sermons on Several Occasions, Complete; containing 141 Sermons, and a Life by the Rev. John Beecham. 2 vols., crown 8vo, 7s. Library Edition. 3 vols., 8vo, 10s. 6d.

Journals of Rev. John Wesley, Complete, with Copious Index. 4 vols., crown 8vo, 10s. Library Edition. 4 vols., demy 8vo, 14s.

Wesley His Own Biographer: Being Selections from the Journals of the Rev. John Wesley, M.A. 648 pp. With 356 Illustrations. Crown 4to, 7s. 6d. Cloth, gilt edges, 8s. 6d.; Half-Morocco, 15s.; Palestine Levant, 17s. 6d.; Crushed Morocco, 35s.

Wesley: The Man, His Teaching, and His Work. Being Sermons and Addresses delivered in City Road Chapel, at the Centenary Commemoration of John Wesley's Death. Revised by the Author. With Portrait of John Wesley. Crown 8vo, 2s. 6d.; Bevelled Boards, gilt edges, 3s. 6d.

The Living Wesley. By the Rev. James H. Rigg, D.D. New Edition. Revised throughout and much enlarged. With Portrait. Crown 8vo, 3s. 6d.

CHARLES H. KELLY, 2, CASTLE STREET, CITY ROAD, E.C.; AND 66, PATERNOSTER ROW, E.C.

THE POPULAR HISTORY OF METHODISM.

CHAPTER I.

PREPARATION FOR METHODISM.

LIFE AT EPWORTH.

The Mother of Methodism.—Methodism received its name in the University of Oxford, but its real birthplace was the nursery of Epworth Rectory. There Susannah Wesley laid the foundation for the Evangelical Revival by her training of John and Charles Wesley. Isaac Taylor said long ago that "the Wesleys' mother was the mother of Methodism," and that verdict is endorsed by all historians. Mrs. Wesley had nineteen children, and her life was a prolonged struggle with straitened means and unfriendly circumstances, yet she approved herself in every relation of life, a wise, brave, devout, tender, noble woman. Her father was Dr. Samuel Annesley, nephew of the first Earl of Anglesea, and Vicar of St. Giles', Cripplegate. After his ejection from his living in 1662, Dr. Annesley became the St. Paul of the Nonconformists. At the age of thirteen his youngest daughter studied the controversy between the Church and the Nonconformists, and decided to cast in her lot with the Church of England.

The Father of the Wesleys.—In 1689 Susannah Annesley married Samuel Wesley, a London curate, with an income of thirty pounds a year, which he doubled by literary work. He also was the son of Nonconformists who had endured persecution and imprisonment for conscience sake. He was actually being trained for their ministry in London when he made up his mind to seek admission to the Church of England, and entered himself as a servitor at Exeter College, Oxford. In the year after his marriage, Samuel Wesley became Rector of South Ormsby, in Lincolnshire, whence he was transferred to Epworth in 1697. Here John Wesley was born on June 17th, 1703, and Charles on December 18th, 1707. Samuel Wesley was a scholar and a poet, but he lacked the practical sagacity and the tact which were essential for dealing with the turbulent Fenmen, among whom he spent nearly forty years. His High Churchism and his Tory principles brought him into sharp contest with his parishioners, who embittered the first twelve years of his residence among them by burning his flax, and by other lawless deeds. He had a life of trouble. He was thrown into Lincoln Castle for debt; two thirds of his parsonage were burned down in 1702, and seven years later it was entirely destroyed by fire. His resources were so straitened that even thirteen years afterwards it was only half furnished.

Mrs. Wesley and her Children.—Such were the struggles with which Susannah Wesley was familiar. Yet she never lost heart or hope. She was a model mother. Her earliest care was to teach her children obedience, for this she regarded as the "only strong and rational foundation of a religious education." The boys and girls were trained to pray by signs before they could speak, and as soon as possible were taught to repeat the Lord's prayer. Truthfulness, good temper, and good manners were insisted on. Mrs. Wesley spared no pains to win the confidence of her children. She was herself their schoolmistress, and had the happy art of fastening her lessons firmly on their memory. She began her work as soon as they were five years old, and all her children, save two or three, learned their letters on the first day. No lesson was ever left till it was mastered. Mrs. Wesley knew the art of repetition and concentration. "It is almost incredible," she says, "what a child may be taught in a quarter of a year by a vigorous application, if it have but a tolerable capacity and good health"

John Wesley's Escape from the Fire.—On February 9th, 1709, the Rectory was totally destroyed by fire. All escaped from the burning house save John Wesley, who was then five years old. Soon after the nurse had rushed from the room he awoke and went to the door, where he found everything in a blaze. He climbed on a chest near the window, and was rescued by two men, one of whom stood on the other's shoulders. Just as the boy was saved the whole roof fell in. The parsonage was burned to the ground in about a quarter of an hour. When his boy was brought to him, the rector cried, "Come, neighbours, let us kneel down; let us give thanks to God! He has given me all my eight children; let the house go; I am rich enough." That rescue from the fire profoundly affected John Wesley. On one of his early portraits, a house in flames is represented with the words, "Is not this a brand plucked out of the fire?"

His Mother's Training.—His mother felt that deliverance a loud call to fresh fidelity. Two years later she wrote in her journal: "I do intend to be more particularly careful of the soul of this child, that Thou hast so mercifully provided for, than ever I have been, that I may do my endeavour to instil into his mind the principles of Thy true religion and virtue. Lord, give me grace to do it sincerely and prudently, and bless my attempts with good success." After the house had been rebuilt, Mrs. Wesley introduced several new features into her training. She taught her children to retire for private Bible reading and prayer. The oldest child took the youngest that could speak, the second in age took the youngest but one, and thus they formed themselves into pairs to read over the evening Psalms with a chapter from the New Testament. Before breakfast they read the morning Psalms and a chapter of the Old Testament. This training shaped the life of John Wesley, and affected the whole course of Methodism. Not less memorable were the moments which Mrs. Wesley spent every evening conversing privately with each of her children "in something that relates to its principal concerns." Years afterwards when he was Fellow of Lincoln, John Wesley wrote to his mother, "If you can spare me only that little part of Thursday evening which you formerly bestowed upon me in another manner, I doubt not but that it would be as useful now for correcting my heart, as it was then in forming my judgment."

SCHOOL AND UNIVERSITY.

Life at Charterhouse.—In 1714, John Wesley entered Charterhouse School on the nomination of the Duke of Buckingham, who had long been his father's friend. Dr. Thomas Walker, under whom Richard Steele and Joseph Addison were trained, was head master, and Wesley soon became one of his favourite scholars. The Lincolnshire boy had many a rough experience at Charterhouse. The elder scholars stole the meat from the smaller lads, so that Wesley says, " From ten to fourteen I had little but bread to eat, and not great plenty of that. I believe this was so far from hurting me, that it laid the foundation of lasting health." Charterhouse made the future Evangelist of England a sound scholar, and thus contributed largely to his influence in later days. In June, 1720, after six years' training, he was elected scholar of Christ Church, Oxford, with an allowance of £40 a year. Charles Wesley went to Westminster School in 1716, where his eldest brother Samuel had been educated, and was afterwards usher. All three brothers were scholars of Christ Church. Old Samuel Wesley was thus justified in his boast that his three sons had received the best education he could get them in England. Methodism owes a great debt to Oxford and to the schools where the Wesleys were trained. The Evangelical Revival would have been a different thing if the Wesleys had not been gentlemen and scholars.

Early Religious Impressions.—As a boy Wesley was so truly serious that he had been admitted by his father to the Communion at the age of eight. He had been strictly educated and carefully taught that he could only be saved " by universal obedience, by keeping all the commandments of God." His removal to a great public school was not without loss. He became much " more negligent than before, even of outward duties, and almost continually guilty of outward sins, which I knew to be such, though they were not scandalous in the eye of the world. However, I still read the Scriptures, and said my prayers, morning and evening. And what I now hoped to be saved by was, (1) not being so bad as other people ; (2) having still a kindness for religion, and (3) reading the Bible, going to church, and saying my prayers."

His first five years at Oxford were of a similar character. He read his Bible and said his prayers, but went on " habitually, and for the most part contentedly, in some or other known sin, indeed, with some intermission and short struggles, especially before and after the Holy Communion," which the rules of his College required him to take three times a year. His scholarship had already won recognition. He delighted in the subtleties of logic, had the finest classical tastes, and the most liberal and manly sentiments. He was " gay and sprightly, with a turn for wit and humour."

A Poor Man's Testimony.—One night a friendly chat with the porter of his college convinced him that there were joys in religion to which he was a stranger. The porter had only one coat, and that day nothing had passed his lips but a drink of water, yet he was full of gratitude. Wesley could not refrain from saying : " You thank God when you have nothing to wear, nothing to eat, and no bed to lie upon. What else do you thank Him for ? " " I thank Him," said the man, " that He has given me my life and being, and a heart to love Him, and a desire to serve Him."

Serious Thoughts.—At the beginning of 1725 Wesley began to think of taking orders. He read Thomas à Kempis' " Imitation of Christ," which taught him that true religion was seated in the heart, and meant purity of thought as well as of word and deed. He was very angry with the writer for being too strict, but his reading bore manifest fruit. Many years later he expressed his opinion that "Thomas à Kempis was next to the Bible." Jeremy Taylor's " Holy Living and Dying," which he studied the same year, led him to make a more exact use of his time. He began to note carefully the employment of every hour. To that habit we owe those journals which still present the most wonderful portrait of himself and his mission that we possess. Wesley was ordained deacon by Bishop Potter in Christ Church Cathedral in September, 1725, and three years later was there admitted to priest's orders by the same prelate. Soon after his ordination in 1725, he preached his first sermon at South Leigh, a village three miles from Witney. In March, 1726, he became Fellow of Lincoln College. He was now a serious and earnest Christian. He wrote to his mother, "Leisure and I have taken leave of one another. I propose to be busy as long as I live, if my health is so long indulged me."

Charles Wesley becomes Serious. — Charles Wesley was resident at Christ Church. But he was still careless about spiritual things, eager chiefly to enjoy himself. When John spoke to him about religion he answered warmly, " What, would you have me to be a saint all at once ? " Whilst John was acting as his father's curate in Lincolnshire in 1729, Charles became more thoughtful. He wrote to consult his brother about keeping a diary, and expressed his hope that he should not relapse into his former state of insensibility. " It is through your means, I firmly believe," he added, " that God will establish what He hath begun in me ; and there is no one person I would so willingly have to be the instrument of good to me as you. It is owing, in great measure, to somebody's prayers (my mother's, most likely) that I am come to think as I do ; for I cannot tell myself how or when I awoke out of my lethargy: only, that it was not long after you went away."

First Converts.—John Wesley had won his first convert in 1725. He and a friend paced the aisles of St. Mary's Church, waiting for the funeral of a young lady whom they had known. Wesley begged that he might have the pleasure of making his companion a whole Christian, to which he said that he knew he was half persuaded already. The friend gladly accepted the counsel, and when he died of consumption, eighteen months later, Wesley was able to rejoice that his words had borne fruit. After Charles Wesley became serious, he helped his next door neighbour, a modest, well-disposed young fellow, who had fallen into vile hands, to break loose from his evil companions. The two young men then attended the weekly Communion together.

OXFORD METHODISM.

The Name " Methodist."—Charles Wesley and two students of kindred spirit formed themselves into a little society. They soon attracted attention. A young gentleman of Christ Church said, " Here is a new sect of Methodists sprung up." The name was quaint, and quickly found its way into every one's mouth. It was not new. It had been applied to an ancient school of physicians, who taught that all diseases might be cured by method in diet and exercise. Other uses of the word might be quoted, but these were temporary, and of minor importance. Now at last it had come to stay. It was not the only name used to describe the little group of friends. They were also styled the Reforming Club, the Godly Club, the Holy Club, Sacramentarians, and Bible Moths. When Wesley returned to Oxford he took the foremost part in the society, and was dubbed Curator or Father of the Holy Club.

A Description of Wesley.—One of the group gives a description of the young Fellow which helps us to understand Wesley's special qualifications as a leader. " Mr. John Wesley was always the chief manager, for which he was very fit ; for he not only had more learning and experience than the rest, but he was blest with such activity as to be always gaining ground, and such steadiness that he lost none. What proposals he made to any, were sure to charm them because they saw him always the same. What supported this uniform vigour was the care he took to consider well of every affair before he engaged in it, making all his decisions in the fear of God, without passion, humour, or self-confidence ; for though he had naturally a very clear apprehension, yet his exact prudence depended more on humanity and singleness of heart. To this I may add that he had, I think, something of authority in his countenance, though, as he did not want address, he could soften his manner, and point it as occasion required. Yet he never assumed anything to himself above his companions. Any of them might speak their mind, and their words were as strictly regarded by him as his by them." To these rules of conduct Wesley was true to the end of his career.

The Oxford Methodists.—The little company of Methodists at first met every Sunday evening, then two nights a week were passed in each other's rooms, and at last every night from six to nine. After opening their meetings with prayer, they studied the Greek Testament and the classics, reviewed the day's work, and consulted about the plans of the morrow. These consultations had special reference to the charities and the Christian work in which they were engaged. They arranged a searching system of self-examination by which all their conduct was brought under review. They fasted on Wednesdays and Fridays, and received the Lord's Supper every week either at their Colleges or at Christ Church. They set themselves to do the will of God in all things, used hourly prayers for some special grace, repeated collects at fixed hours, had stated times for meditation and private prayer, and were always seeking to do good to the bodies and souls of those about them.

An Irish Methodist.—A young Irishman called Morgan led the way in those labours for the outcast which bore such fruit in early Methodist history. In August, 1730, Morgan visited a murderer lying under sentence of death at the jail, and spoke to the debtors who were confined there. He saw what a fine opportunity of doing good awaited them here, and spoke about it so often that at last the Wesleys went with him to the Castle. What they saw made them as enthusiastic as Morgan. They now resolved to visit the prisoners once or twice a week. Not content with such labours, they also undertook to look after the sick in any parish where the clergyman was willing to accept their help. Samuel Wesley had himself visited the prisoners when he was an undergraduate at Oxford, and greatly approved of the work his sons were doing. The Bishop of Oxford's chaplain, who had the spiritual care of any condemned prisoners, heartily welcomed their help, and told them how pleased the bishop himself was with their zeal. The Holy Club was small. A year after John Wesley became its head there were only five members, and it probably never had more than nine. The young Methodists had to suffer much reproach. But their father told them, " I question whether a mortal can arrive to a higher degree of perfection than steadily to do good, and for that very reason patiently and meekly to suffer evil. Bear no more sail than is necessary, but steer steady." Morgan died of consumption in August, 1732, but his influence still lives in Methodism. The historian Mr. J. R. Green says, " The noblest result of the religious revival was the steady attempt, which has never ceased from that day to this, to remedy the guilt, the ignorance, the physical suffering, the social degradation of the profligate and the poor." In such work Morgan was the pioneer.

George Whitefield.—On the eve of their departure for Georgia a notable recruit cast in his lot with the Oxford Methodists. George Whitefield's father kept the Bell Inn at Gloucester, and after his death, the young fellow helped his mother and brother in the inn. A friend often entreated him to go to Oxford, but it was not till an old schoolfellow, who was a servitor at Pembroke College, called at the house, that the way seemed to open. In 1728 he went up to the University as servitor at Pembroke College. He was surrounded by careless and riotous young fellows, who jeered at him for taking the Sacrament at St. Mary's on a week-day. He had long admired the devotion of the little company of Methodists, and wished greatly to join them, but he had no means of gaining an introduction. It came in an unexpected way. An old woman in the workhouse having tried to commit suicide, Whitefield sent word to Charles Wesley, giving the messenger strict orders not to mention his name. Happily she did not obey, and Charles Wesley invited Whitefield to breakfast next morning. Whitefield was longing for some spiritually-minded friends, who might encourage and strengthen him. He says: "Charles Wesley soon discovered this, and, like a wise winner of souls, made all his discourses turn that way. And when he put into my hands Franke's *Treatise against the Fear of Man*, and *The Country Parson's Advice to his Parishioners*, I took my leave. In a short time he let me have another book, entitled *The Life of God in the Soul of Man*, and though I had fasted, and watched, and prayed, and received the Sacrament so long, yet I never knew what true religion was, till God sent me that excellent treatise, by the hands of my never-to-be-forgotten friend." Whitefield at once joined the Society, with results which profoundly affected the whole history of Methodism.

Wesley's Generosity.—In his life at Oxford, Wesley showed that self-sacrificing generosity which marked his whole course. One winter's day a young girl for whose schooling the Holy Club provided, came into his room. Her linen gown and half-starved look made him enquire if she had no more suitable attire. When he found that she had not, he put his hand in his pocket. He had scarcely any money. He looked on his pictures, and bitterly reproached himself with spending money on luxuries, while such distress lay at his door. Henceforth he husbanded his resources that he might succour those in need. His income was only thirty pounds at first, but he lived on twenty-eight pounds, and gave away two. As his income increased he kept his expenses down to the same amount, and in the fourth year was able to give away £94. He paid the mistress of a little school, and clothed some, if not all, of its twenty scholars.

Wesley's Reputation.—Meanwhile Wesley was steadily gaining influence in University circles. He preached before the University in 1733 and 1734. He was lecturer at Lincoln College in Logic, Greek, and Philosophy. His skill in logic was specially recognized, and the experience gained as Moderator in the disputations at his own college proved of unspeakable value in the controversies of later life. "For several years," he says, "I was Moderator in the disputations which were held six times a week at Lincoln College in Oxford. I could not avoid acquiring hereby some degree of expertness in arguing, and especially in discerning and pointing out well-covered and plausible fallacies. I have since found abundant reason to praise God for giving me this honest art. By this, when men have hedged me in by what they call demonstrations, I have been many times able to dash them in pieces, in spite of all its covers, to touch the very point where the fallacy lay; and it flew open in a moment." Besides his University honours, Wesley found recognition in a wider sphere, being chosen a member of the Society for the Propagation of Christian Knowledge in 1732.

FINAL STAGE OF PREPARATION.

Mission to Georgia.—After their father's death on April 25th, 1735, the Wesleys resolved to devote themselves to work in Georgia. They sailed for Savannah on October 21st, with their friends Benjamin Ingham and Charles Delamotte. Susannah Wesley had expressed her hearty approval. "Had I twenty sons, I should rejoice if they were all so employed." John Wesley was moved by a strong desire to work out his own salvation, and a longing to preach Christ to the Indians. He was sent out by the Society for the Propagation of the Gospel, who allowed him fifty pounds a year. His brother Charles was secretary to General Oglethorpe, the Governor of the Colony, who had been a friend and correspondent of the Rector of Epworth. The mission was a sore disappointment to the Wesleys. They had hoped to escape the pomp and show of the world, but found themselves in the midst of intrigue and worldliness. Charles Wesley had some bitter experiences at Frederika, where the settlers slandered him to the governor, robbed him of the commonest comforts, and even plotted against his life. After six months of misery, he returned in broken health to England. John Wesley remained in the Colony for nearly two years, but was at last driven home by the plots of his enemies.

Wesley in Savannah. — His uncompromising High Churchism had aroused strong animosity. He insisted on dipping infants three times in the font, inculcated fasting, confession, and weekly communion, refused the Lord's Supper to all who had not been baptized by an episcopally ordained minister, and would not bury any who were not duly baptized according to the forms of the Church of England. Eleven or twelve years after his return he received a letter from a devout Moravian. He says: "What a truly Christian piety and simplicity breathe in these lines! And yet this very man, when I was at Savannah, did I refuse to admit to the Lord's Table, because he was not baptized; that is, not baptized by a minister who had been episcopally ordained. Can anyone carry High Church zeal higher than this? And how well have I since been beaten with my own staff!" The unrest caused by his own intolerance came to a climax through his refusal to admit a young married lady to the communion. Wesley had been greatly attracted by Miss Hopkey before her marriage, but his Moravian friends were strongly opposed to the union, and he yielded to their judgment. After her marriage to Mr. Williamson, he told her

of some points in her behaviour which he considered blame-
worthy, and when the lady failed to amend he repelled her from
the communion. This exercise of discipline brought a storm
on his head, and he found it wise to leave Savannah in
December, 1737.

Influence of the Moravians.—Wesley's mission to Georgia
was part of his providential training for his life-work. He had
been greatly impressed on the voyage to America by the
conduct of his Moravian fellow-passengers, whose humility and
devotion, and above all their fearlessness in the Atlantic gales,
showed him the reality of their faith in Christ. When he
landed in Georgia a Moravian minister asked him some searching questions as to the witness of the Spirit and saving faith,
which made him vaguely uneasy about his own state. He
spent much time with the Moravian settlers in Georgia, and
attended their Sunday evening service, "not as a teacher, but
a learner." On his return voyage he found that he had not
the faith which saves from fear. He set down in his journal
many bitter things about himself. He had learnt in the ends
of the earth that he had fallen short of the glory of God, and
that his own works, sufferings, and righteousness, so far from
reconciling him to God, needed an atonement themselves, or
they could not abide God's righteous judgment. He had gone
out to teach the Georgian Indians the nature of Christianity, but
says, "What have I learned myself in the meantime? Why
(what I the least of all suspected) that I who went to America
to convert others, was never myself converted to God." In
later years he revised this harsh judgment in some notes
appended to it in his journals. He saw that he had even then
the faith of a servant, though not that of a son.

The Wesleys Find Rest.—On his return to London,
Wesley met a Moravian minister, Peter Böhler, who was on
his way to Georgia. Through conversation with him, he was
at last convinced of the want of saving faith. His brother
Charles had also reached the same point, and both were now
earnestly seeking rest. Charles Wesley found the blessing on
Whit Sunday, May 21st, 1738, and on the following Wednesday,
whilst listening to Luther's preface to the Epistle to the
Romans, where the reformer describes the change wrought in
the heart through faith in Christ, Wesley says, "I felt my
heart strangely warmed. I felt I did trust in Christ, Christ
alone, for salvation; and an assurance was given me, that He
had taken away *my* sins, even *mine*, and saved *me* from the law
of sin and death." He was escorted by a little triumphal
party of friends to the lodgings, in Little Britain, where Charles
Wesley lay sick, and declared "I believe." Charles had already
written a hymn on his own conversion, which the company

sang with great joy. It was a Te Deum for the grace that had made them the children of God.

> Oh, how shall I the goodness tell,
>   Father, which Thou to me hast showed?
> That I, a child of wrath and hell,
>   I should be called a child of God,
> Should know, should feel my sins forgiven,
> Blest with this antepast of heaven!

But the hymn was more than a Te Deum. We hear in it the first of those invitations to the outcast, which were the glory of the Evangelical Revival.

> Outcasts of men, to you I call,
>   Harlots, and publicans, and thieves!
> He spreads His arms to embrace you all;
>   Sinners alone His grace receives;
> No need of Him the righteous have;
> He comes the lost to seek and save.

CHAPTER II.

THE EVANGELIST OF ENGLAND.

THE GREAT AWAKENING.

The Eve of the Evangelical Revival.—The change in the Wesleys gave no small offence to their old friends, but they calmly stood their ground. John Wesley visited the Moravian settlement at Herrnhuth on the border of Bohemia, where he met so many living witnesses to the power of faith, that he gained new confidence. All his doubts vanished. On his return to London he preached in the churches, and expounded the Scriptures in the Religious Societies which had sprung up in connexion with the Church of England in London and Westminster.

State of England.—The hour was ripe for the Evangelical Revival. Southey says, " there never was less religious feeling, either within the Establishment or without, than when Wesley blew his trumpet, and awakened those who slept." We learn from James Hutton that the Religious Societies had settled down into lifelessness. Isaac Taylor says, " Nonconformity seemed likely soon to be found nowhere but in books." Bishop Burnet's candidates for ordination were scandalously ignorant of the Bible. Dr. Secker asserts in his Charge of 1738, that " an open and professed disregard to religion is become, through a variety of unhappy causes, the distinguishing character of the present age ; that this evil is grown to a great height in the metropolis of the nation, and is daily spreading through every part of it."

He says it had already brought in " such dissoluteness and contempt of principle in the higher part of the world, and such profligate intemperance and fearlessness of committing crimes in the lower, as must, if this torrent of iniquity stop not, become absolutely fatal." Gin drinking had spread like an epidemic. Every sixth house in London was a grog-shop. The London doctors in 1750 stated that there were fourteen thousand cases of illness, directly attributable to the mania for gin drinking. The state of the working classes in Newcastle-on-Tyne, in Kingswood and in the great industrial and mining centres was appalling.

Field Preaching.—It was George Whitefield, who made the first active assault on the irreligion of the day. Whilst the Wesleys were in America he had been ordained, and had won great popularity as a preacher. When he visited Bristol in 1739 he was shut out from the pulpits of the churches. He felt, however, that he had a message to deliver, and on February 17th, 1739, ventured to preach to the Kingswood colliers in the open-air. He soon had congregations numbering ten to twenty thousand people. A large bowling green in the heart of Bristol was set at his service, and enormous congregations gathered to hear him. For six weeks he continued his work. Then he begged Wesley to leave London and take his place. Wesley was very busy in the metropolis, but his friend's importunity conquered. On April 1st, he stood in Whitefield's congregation. "I could scarce reconcile myself at first," he says, " to this strange way of preaching in the fields, of which he set me an example on Sunday; having been all my life (till very lately) so tenacious of every point relating to decency and order, that I should have thought the saving of souls almost a sin if it had not been done in a church." On Monday afternoon Wesley "submitted to be more vile " by preaching in the open air to three thousand people from the words " The Spirit of the Lord is upon me, because He hath anointed me to preach the Gospel to the poor." He was now fairly launched. For ten weeks he remained in Bristol preaching four times a Sunday, and holding service almost every day of the week.

First Methodist Chapel.—The work prospered and on May 12th, 1739, the foundation stones of the first Methodist Chapel in the world were laid in the Horse Fair, Bristol. It was intended to provide room for two religious societies that met in the city. Wesley had to take on himself, the whole responsibility of finding funds, but he had absolute confidence in the help of God, and " set out, nothing doubting." The chapel which has a memorable Methodist history is still standing in Broadmead.

Open-air Services in London.—The chief triumphs of early Methodism were won in its open-air services. When Wesley returned to London, in June, 1739 he preached to Whitefield's congregation of twelve or fourteen thousand people on Blackheath. At Upper Moorfields and Kennington Common on the following Sunday he had similar crowds. Charles Wesley now followed his brother's example, so that the three friends were all enlisted in this work. The churches were closed against them, but no one could rob them of an audience. It is easy to see in this the hand of God. No churches could possibly hold the crowds that wished to hear the Gospel message, and people who would never have ventured inside a church, were attracted to these novel services. Wesley nobly vindicates his method as a field-preacher in his *Appeals to Men of Reason and Religion.* He speaks of the multitudes in Kingswood and around Newcastle, "who, week after week, spent the Lord's Day, either in the ale-house, or in idle diversions, and never troubled themselves about going to church, or any public worship at all. Had the minister of the parish preached like an angel, it had profited them nothing, for they heard him not. But when one came and said, 'Yonder is a man preaching on the top of the mountain,' they ran in droves to hear what he would say, and God spoke to their hearts. It is hard to conceive anything else which could have reached them. Had it not been for field-preaching, the uncommonness of which was the very circumstance that recommended it, they must have run on in the error of their way and perished in their blood." He dwells upon the hardships of the field-preacher, the summer sun, and the wintry rain or wind. Yet these were small trials. "Far beyond all these, are the contradiction of sinners, the scoffs both of the great vulgar, and the small; contempt and reproach of every kind; often more than verbal affronts, stupid, brutal violence, sometimes to the hazard of health, or limbs, or life. Brethren, do you envy us this honour? What, I pray, would buy you to be a field-preacher? Or what, think you, could induce any man of common sense to continue therein one year, unless he had a full conviction in himself that it was the will of God concerning him?"

London Methodism.—On November 11th, 1739, Wesley preached in the old Foundery in Moorfields. A serious explosion which occurred here in 1716 had led to the removal of the Royal Arsenal to Woolwich. In 1739, two gentlemen, who up to that time were strangers to Wesley, asked him to preach here. A lease was taken, and the old buildings were repaired and galleries added. The place became the head quarters of Methodism until City Road Chapel was opened in 1778. It would seat fifteen hundred people, and had a band-room behind in which classes and prayer-meetings were held. One end of this was fitted up as a school-room, the other formed the first Book-room for the sale of Methodist publications. Above the band-room were Wesley's apartments, and at the end of the chapel a house for his preachers. There was also a coach-house and stable. Wesley was now able to provide a home for his own Society. The first members met at Fetter Lane, but erroneous teaching had crept in there, and at last, in July 1740, Wesley was compelled to withdraw from that Society with the seventy-five members who were not carried away by the Moravian teaching. These were now joined to the members at the Foundery. The controversies at Fetter Lane had been a sore hindrance to the work in London, but henceforth there was steady and rapid progress. On February 1st, 1742 there were eleven hundred members in the London Society.

The Methodist Society.—Wesley had always recognised Christian fellowship as a fundamental necessity for those who wished to serve God. Oxford Methodism itself, was based upon this principle. An earnest man, whom Wesley took a long journey to visit in those days, told him, " Sir, you are to serve God and go to heaven. Remember you cannot serve Him alone ; the Bible knows nothing of solitary religion." On his voyage to America, in Savannah, and on his return to England, Wesley steadily acted on this counsel. When he became a field preacher he found daily illustration of its vital importance. At the end of 1739 eight or ten people who were earnestly seeking Christ, begged Wesley to guide them. It soon became impossible for him to visit their homes. He therefore arranged to meet them every Thursday evening, when he gave them counsel and closed with "prayer suitable to their necessities."

Methodist Finance.—At Bristol similar arrangements were made. The debt on the chapel there was heavy. On February 15th, 1742, Captain Foy suggested that each member should pay a penny a week till it was removed. Many, it was said, were too poor to give even this amount. The Captain replied, " then put eleven of the poorest with me ; and if they can give anything, well : I will call on them weekly ; and if they can give nothing, I will give for them as well as myself. And each of you call on eleven of your neighbours weekly ; receive what they can give, and make up what is wanting." The person who received contributions was the leader, and his company formed a class. The leaders got to know their own members well. Sometimes they reported to Wesley grave faults of conduct which they had discovered. He saw at once that here was a missing link. The leaders were instructed to make careful inquiry as to the conduct of those whom they visited. Many "disorderly walkers" were thus discovered, some of whom were restored, and others put out of the Society. The new organisation was quickly introduced into other places. What had been a purely financial arrangement thus secured for Methodism a lay pastorate, by whose means the whole membership was brought under wise and godly oversight, and divided into classes, which met together every week for prayer and fellowship. Wesley says, "It can scarce be conceived what advantages have been reaped from this little prudential regulation." Many now happily experienced that Christian fellowship, of which they had not so much as an idea before. They began to "bear one another's burdens," and naturally to "care for each other." Nothing did more to make Methodism a mighty spiritual force, than its class meetings. The quarterly visitation of the classes by the preachers began in London in 1742, as also did the custom of giving the members a ticket with a verse of scripture on it. By the use of this ticket improper persons were kept from intruding into the private meetings of the Society. A select Society or Band for more advanced Christians was also formed, and had its own special tickets. Lovefeasts, which Wesley had kept with his Moravian friends, were also introduced into the Methodist system.

Rules of the Society. Rules for the Society were drawn up by the Wesleys in 1743, which are still given to those who are admitted as members. It will be seen how wide the gateway is :

"There is only one condition previously required in those who desire admission into these Societies ; *viz., a desire to flee from the wrath to come, to be saved from their sins.*" But wherever this is really fixed in the soul it will be shown by its fruits. It is therefore expected of all who continue therein, that they should continue to evidence their desire of salvation,

FIRST, by doing no harm, by avoiding evil in every kind; especially that which is most generally practised. Such is—

The taking the name of God in vain :

The profaning the day of the Lord, either by doing ordinary work thereon, or by buying or selling :

Drunkenness; *buying or selling spirituous liquors*, or *drinking them*, unless in cases of extreme necessity :

Fighting, quarrelling, brawling; brother *going to law* with brother; returning *evil for evil*, or *railing for railing;* the *using many words* in buying or selling;

The *buying* or *selling uncustomed goods ;*

The *giving or taking things on usury ; i.e.* unlawful interest.

Uncharitable or unprofitable conversation; particularly speaking evil of Magistrates or of Ministers:

Doing to others as we would not they should do unto us :

Doing what we know is not for the glory of God ; as,—

The *putting on of gold or costly apparel ;*

The *taking such diversions* as cannot be used in the name of the LORD JESUS;

The *singing* those *songs*, or *reading* those *books* which do not tend to the knowledge or love of GOD:

Softness, and needless self-indulgence:

Laying up treasures upon earth:

Borrowing without a probability of paying; or taking up goods without a probability of paying for them.

It is expected of all who continue in these Societies, that they should continue to evidence their desire of salvation,

SECONDLY, by doing good, by being in every kind merciful after their power; as they have opportunity, doing good of every possible sort, and as far as possible, to all men:

To their bodies, of the ability that God giveth, by giving food to the hungry, by clothing the naked, by visiting or helping them that are sick or in prison:

To their souls, by instructing, *reproving,* or exhorting all they have any intercourse with; trampling under foot that enthusiastic doctrine of devils, that "we are not to do good, unless *our heart be free to it.*"

By doing good especially to them that are of the household of faith, or groaning so to be; employing them preferably to others, buying one of another, helping each other in business; and so much the more, because the world will love its own, and them *only.*

By all possible *diligence* and *frugality,* that the Gospel be not blamed.

By running with patience the race that is set before them, *denying themselves, and taking up their cross daily;* submitting to bear the reproach of Christ; to be as the filth and offscouring of the world; and looking that men should *say all manner of evil of them falsely, for the Lord's sake.*

It is expected of all who desire to continue in these Societies, that they should continue to evidence their desire of salvation,

THIRDLY, by attending upon all the ordinances of God: such are,—

The public worship of God;

The ministry of the word, either read or expounded;

The Supper of the Lord;

Family and private prayer;

Searching the Scriptures; and

Fasting or abstinence.

These are the General Rules of our Societies: all which we are taught of God to observe, even in His written word, the only rule, and the sufficient rule, both of our faith and practice. And all these we know His Spirit writes on every truly awakened heart. If there be any among us who observe them not, who habitually break any of them, let it be made known unto them who watch over that soul, as they that must give an account. We will admonish him of the error of his ways: we will bear with him for a season. But then if he repent not, he hath no more place among us. We have delivered our own souls.

JOHN WESLEY.

May 1, 1743. CHARLES WESLEY."

Wesley gloried in the catholicity of his test of membership. When he visited Glasgow in 1788, after preaching three times, he gave a short account of Methodism, "particularly insisting on the circumstances—There is no other religious Society under heaven, which requires nothing of men in order to their admission into it, but a desire to save their souls. Look all around you, you cannot be admitted into the Church, or Society of the Presbyterians, Anabaptists, Quakers, or any others, unless you hold the same opinions with them, and adhere to the same mode of worship.

The Methodists alone do not insist on your holding this or that opinion ; but they think and let think. Neither do they impose any particular mode of worship ; but you may continue to worship in your former manner, be it what it may. Now, I do not know any other religious Society, either ancient or modern, wherein such liberty of conscience is now allowed, or has been allowed, since the age of the Apostles. Here is our glorying ; and a glorying peculiar to us. What Society shares it with us ? "

EXTENSION OF WESLEY'S FIELD.

Wesley in Newcastle-on-Tyne.—Up till 1742 the influence of Methodism was almost confined to London and Bristol. But in that year Wesley visited Newcastle-on-Tyne. As he walked through the town, he says, "I was surprised : so much drunkenness, cursing, and swearing (even from the mouths of little children) do I never remember to have seen and heard before, in so small a compass of time. Surely this place is ripe for Him 'who came not to call the righteous, but sinners to repentance.' " On his first Sunday he had an audience which outnumbered even those which gathered to hear him in Moorfields. The people gave him a welcome, such as he had never had before. Wesley and his brother were now frequent visitors. He had never seen a work of God so evenly and gradually carried on. Before the year was out a new preaching place was begun with only twenty-six shillings in hand. A Quaker came to Wesley's help with a note for one hundred pounds. He was able to preach in the shell of the house on March 25th, 1743. The Orphan House, as it was called, became the Methodist head-quarters in the North, and had a wonderful history.

The Epworth Awakening.—As Wesley returned from his first visit to Newcastle, he found his way to Epworth. The curate would not allow him to preach in the church, but he stayed for a week in the town, preaching every night on his father's tomb, and visiting the neighbouring villages. Some of the most beautiful and touching scenes of the Great Revival are associated with those churchyard services. When Wesley preached his last sermon the people hung on his lips for nearly three hours, and even then they scarcely knew how to let him go. The harvest of many years painful sowing had come. Wesley says, "Oh, let none think his labour of love is lost

because the fruit does not immediately appear.   Near forty
years did my father labour here ; but he saw little fruit of his
labour.   I took some pains among this people, too ; and my
strength also seemed spent in vain.   But now the fruit
appeared.   There were scarce any in the town on whom
either my father or I had taken any pains formerly, but the
seed sown so long since now sprung up, bringing forth repentance and remission of sins."   Such was the joyful news which
Wesley bore to his mother's death bed.   She died at the
Foundery three days after his return, rejoicing that God had
answered her prayers and crowned the work of her husband,
herself and her family, with results infinitely beyond their
hopes.

Rapid Progress.—After the great extension to Newcastle
in May 1742, Methodism began to spread over England.   John
Nelson, who had been converted under Wesley's preaching in
London, returned to his home at Birstall to spread the Methodist
leaven.   Birstall itself became a changed place.   Many of the
greatest profligates, and most abandoned drunkards were
converted.   Wesley visited Nelson on his way to and from
Newcastle, and the work soon spread into the West Riding of
Yorkshire.   During the year many societies were formed in
Somerset, Wilts, Gloucestershire, Leicestershire, Warwickshire,
Nottinghamshire and the South of Yorkshire.   The same
summer Charles Wesley visited Wednesbury, Leeds, and
Newcastle.   Next year he introduced Methodism to Cornwall.
Redruth was " taken," according to his graphic word.   God
gave him the hearts of the tinners, who said if any man spoke
against the Methodists he deserved to be stoned.   Such an
impression was made, that a fortnight after Charles
returned, John Wesley set out with his preachers, Nelson and
Downes, to carry on the campaign.   The physical discomforts
were great, for the preachers had to lie on the floor, and
found it hard to get a meal.   Wesley quaintly gave
thanks that the skin was off one side only, and told
his companion, Brother Nelson, "we ought to be thankful
that there are plenty of blackberries, for this is the best
country I ever saw for getting an appetite, but the worst for
getting food.   Do the people think we live by preaching ? "

West London Methodism.— On May 29th, 1743,
Wesley preached for the first time in West Street Chapel,
Seven Dials, which now became his West End Centre.   The
London Society numbered 1,950 members, and arrangements
were made by which they were divided into three parts, so
that there should not be more than six hundred at one
Sacramental service.   The chapel had been built for the
Huguenots, and their Communion cups are still used at Great

Queen Street. West Street has a memorable Methodist history. John and Charles Wesley, Whitefield, and Fletcher occupied its pulpit, the Countess of Huntingdon and her aristocratic friends sat in its pews, multitudes of anxious inquirers flocked to the services. It gave Methodism a home in the West End, and proved the fruitful mother of other churches and societies. It is still standing, but it passed out of Methodist hands in 1798, when Great Queen Street became its successor.

Methodism in Ireland.—In the summer of 1747, one of the preachers called Thomas Williams, came to Dublin, where he had such success that Wesley crossed over to help him. On August 9th, he landed in Dublin. Here he found that a Society of two hundred and eighty members had been gathered. The people listened eagerly to his message, and Wesley thought that if he or his brother could have been there for a few months there might have been a Society as large as that in London. Two weeks after Wesley's departure, Charles arrived with his friend Mr. Charles Perronet. The mob was now turning all its strength against the Methodists. Papists and Protestants combined in the assault, and there were many cases of violence. Charles Wesley spent six months of great success in Ireland. Then his brother arrived, and made a tour among the country towns, preaching to vast congregations. The Methodist preachers visited Cork, where the awakening became even more general than it had been in Newcastle. When Charles Wesley came in August, 1748, he was received as an angel of God. One Sunday his congregation on the marsh numbered more than ten thousand. Protestants and Papists, high and low, received him with the utmost good-will, and hung upon his words. Next year came the era of the mob, when the Methodists scarcely dared to venture into the streets, and the grand jury actually found a bill against Charles Wesley as "a person of ill-fame, a vagabond, and a common disturber of His Majesty's peace, and prayed that he might be transported." The work in Ireland was at first more wide than deep, but though many proved fickle, multitudes were brought, as Wesley says, "from darkness to light, from serving the devil, to serve the living God." Wesley gave more than six years of his life to Ireland, and crossed the Channel forty-two times in order to labour there.

Methodism in Scotland.—Wesley paid his first visit to Scotland in 1751. Some of John Haime's dragoons had founded Societies in Dundee and Musselborough, and a colonel in the latter town urged Wesley to visit the place. Whitefield advised him not to go as his Arminian principles would "leave him nothing to do but to dispute from morning till night." Wesley replied that he would go, but would studiously avoid controverted points, and keep to the fundamental truths of the Gospel. He had a large congregation at Musselborough, who listened with breathless attention to the evangelist. Prejudices which had been taking root for years, were plucked up in an hour. Wesley was urged to stay a few days, but his engagements called him away. His companion, Christopher Hopper, however returned, and a good work began in Scotland. Wesley paid many visits in after years. In 1766 he was at Glasgow, where, as he spoke plainly about their prejudices, he says, " Shame, concern, and a mixture of various passions, were painted on their faces; and I perceived the Scots, if you touch but the right key, receive as lively impressions as the English." He found that though the people were well grounded in their catechism, many of them were " wholly unacquainted with true religion, yea, and all genuine morality."

WESLEY'S HELPERS AND ITINERANT LIFE.

Lay-Preachers.—It would have been impossible for the Wesleys to enter all the doors which opened to them after the field preaching began, had not a band of lay-preachers been raised up as their helpers. Wesley's prejudices against such methods were very strong, and when Thomas Maxfield, whom he had left in London to meet the members at the Foundery during his own absence, began to preach, he hurried back to town to stop the irregularity. His mother saw his trouble, and when he told her how he felt, she made the notable reply: " John, take care what you do with respect to that young man, for he is as surely called of God to preach as you are. Examine what have been the fruits of his preaching, and hear him yourself." Wesley followed that sagacious counsel, and was compelled to say: ' It is the Lord ; let Him do what seemeth Him good.' He was soon provided with a noble band of helpers. John Nelson, the Birstall stonemason, won from Southey the tribute that he " had as high a spirit and as brave a heart as ever Englishman was blessed with." John Downes, the mathematical genius ; Thomas Walsh, the noted Hebrew Scholar ; Thomas Olivers, hymnist and controversialist—these were some of Wesley's first helpers, whose names are still cherished in Methodism. Their histories given in the " Early Methodist Preachers " rank among the classics of the Evangelical Revival.

The Preacher's Horse.—The early Methodist preacher would have been utterly unable to get round his vast circuit without his faithful horse. When Thomas Olivers set out for Cornwall in 1743, at Mr. Wesley's request, he had no money to buy a horse, and carried his saddle-bags with his books, and his linen over his shoulder. A friend asked why he had not a horse, and offered to pay for one. For five pounds he purchased a colt about two-and-a-half years old, on which he travelled a hundred thousand miles, during the next quarter of a century. The memorial of that faithful friend still stands in Olivers' Autobiography. " In this also I see the hand of God : for I parted with one horse, rather than bring reproach on the Gospel ; and, as a reward, He provided me such another as, in many respects, none of my brethren could ever boast of." We understand what this meant, when we find another preacher compelled to walk twelve hundred miles one winter and spring, because his horse had fallen sick. The Minutes of 1765 show us that the horse claimed his share of attention in Conference. It was asked, " Are all the preachers merciful to their beasts ? " The answer was " Perhaps not. Everyone ought—1. Never to ride hard. 2. To see with his own eyes his horse rubbed, fed, and bedded."

Kingswood School.—Wesley's life in Oxford, and in Georgia shows what profound interest he felt in Christian education. In 1739, a school was built for the colliers' children at Kingswood. Wesley hoped to make Kingswood a truly Christian school, for the benefit of Methodism in general, and several of his people sent their children. In 1748 the place was enlarged and solemnly opened. The colliers' school was still maintained, though a new school had sprung up beside it. Rules were prepared and an annual collection, which has been continued ever since, was made through the Societies for the work. Wesley prepared text books, and spared no pains to make it a success, but his rules were too severe, and his officers were not well chosen. The place was a sore disappointment to him. In 1794 it became a school for preachers' sons only, and in that capacity has had a distinguished history. It has sent to the Universities a long succession of brilliant scholars, who have won the highest distinction. In 1851 the school was removed to Lansdown Hill, near Bath. The school for ministers' daughters at Southport was founded by the munificence of Mr. Fernley.

Wesley's Conference.—Wesley's first Conference was held at the Foundery in the last days of June, 1744. Besides John and Charles Wesley, there were four clergymen, and four " lay brethren" present. How to regulate the doctrine, discipline and practice of Methodism, was the subject for discussion. The first two days were given to the consideration of justi-. fication, faith, sanctification and other doctrinal subjects, on the third day, the relation of Methodism to the Church of England was discussed. The organisation of the new society was carefully considered on the last three days of the week. It was held that " lay assistants" were only allowable in cases of necessity. The famous " Twelve Rules of a Helper," which are still cherished as the marching orders of Methodist Preachers were now drawn up.

The Conference became a recognized annual gathering, which knit the workers together, and furnished an invaluable opportunity for discussing everything that concerned the preachers and the United Societies. Doctrine assumed a prominent place in the early Conferences, but as the work broadened out, and the doctrinal standards were fixed, the oversight of the growing organisation occupied more and more fully the attention of the Conference.

Wesley's Itinerancy.—Wesley's labours are simply astonishing. Mr. Lecky says: "He was gifted with a frame of iron, and with energies that never flagged." During his long itinerancy, he paid more turnpike toll than any man who ever lived. He travelled about five thousand miles a year, and is said to have preached 40,500 sermons. His active life began before his evangelical conversion. When at Oxford, he travelled 1050 miles in one year to preach in the village churches around the University. In the beginning of the great revival he rode on horseback sometimes as much as ninety miles a day. It was not till 1773 that he began regularly to use a carriage. His journals are crowded with incidents which bring his itinerant life before us. He had not a few accidents, and was out in many terrible storms. Nothing was allowed to interfere with his programme of work. Notice had to be given beforehand of his route, and people flocked to hear him, so that he knew what disappointment any failure to keep his plan would cause.

Wesley's Journals.—The great authority for the history of Methodism is Wesley's journals. They were published in twenty-one parts, stretching from the time when he sailed from Georgia to within six months of his death. Mr. Augustine Birrell, Q.C., M.P., recently described these journals as "the most amazing record of human exertion ever penned by man." The contrast between George Fox's journal and Wesley's, is very striking. The Quaker is absorbed in his own religious experiences, and the labours and sufferings of his co-religionists. The Methodist is a man of open eyes and ears—the greatest traveller, the keenest observer, and one of the most variously read men that England produced in the eighteenth century. How vividly human John Wesley was, no one knows till they read his journals. He is, first of all, the Evangelist of England, the central figure in the greatest awakening that ever moved this country, but he is also a man of infinite curiosity and most amiable credulity, a true lover of his kind. The journals are not only the best history of the Evangelical Revival and of Wesley's life, they are also a storehouse of information about the England of the eighteenth century, its modes of travel, the hardships and perils of the road, the aspect of English towns, the characteristics of English society. It is not easy to say how far they contributed towards the spread of real intelligence among the early Methodists. Critiques of books and judgments on historic characters are intermingled with notes on art and natural history, descriptions of scenery, of famous gardens and rising English towns. There are few books so profoundly instructive and so deeply interesting as these records of the busiest and most useful man of his time. Coleridge felt the charm of Southey's *Wesley* so keenly, that of all the volumes in his "ragged book regiment," these were oftenest in his hands, and he was wont to resort to them whenever sickness or languor made him feel the need of an old friend. Edward Fitzgerald had the same feeling about Wesley's *Journal*. He describes it as "one of the most interesting books in the language; well worth reading and having, not only as an outline of Wesley's own singular character, but of the conditions of England, Ireland, and Scotland in the last century. . . . Curious to think of this Diary of Wesley's running almost coevally with Walpole's Letter-Diary—the two men born and dying, too, within a few years of one another, and with such different lives to record. . . . If you have not read the little Autobiography of Wesley's disciple, John Nelson, give a shilling for it. It seems to me something wonderful to read these books, written in a style that cannot alter, because natural; . . . remarkable to read, pure, unaffected, and undying English, while Addison and Johnson are tainted with a style which all the world imitated."

The Mob.—The early Methodists had to endure much persecution, both from the mob and the magistrate. Staffordshire was especially noted for its fierce opposition. In June, 1743, there was a terrible riot in Wednesbury, which lasted six days. When Wesley visited the sufferers in October, 1743, the mob beset the house, and compelled him to go with them to the magistrate. For five hours, amid rain and darkness, he was surrounded by furious rioters from Wednesbury and Walsall, but he was as calm and self-possessed as though he had been sitting in his study. The woman who led the Wednesbury mob became his champion, and the captain of the Walsall rioters also took his part. "Sir," he said, "I will spend my life for you. Follow me, and not one soul here shall touch a hair of your head." He was wonderfully preserved. He only lost one flap of his waistcoat and a little skin off one of his hands. A man struck repeatedly at the back of his head with a large oak stick, but he always missed his mark. When he reached Nottingham after this terrible experience, Charles Wesley said: "My brother came, delivered out of the mouth of the lions ! He *looked* like a soldier of Christ. His clothes were torn to tatters." His conduct on that night led honest Munchin, the captain of the Walsall rioters to join the Society. He knew how to appreciate a true hero. When Charles met him five days after the riot, he asked Munchin what he thought of his brother. " Think of him," said he, " that he is a man of God, and God was on his side, when so many of us could not kill one man ? "

Days of Peril.—Charles Wesley had already had experience of the Cornish mob, whose passions were inflamed by the violent sermons against the Methodists which they heard in the Parish Churches. At Falmouth, in July, 1745, John Wesley had to face a serious riot. When the sailors burst into the house where he was, he followed his rule—"always to look a mob in the face,"—and soon made the rioters ashamed of their conduct. Wesley did not receive a single blow. He says: "I never saw before, not at Walsall itself, the hand of God so plainly as here." Next year he was in great peril from a mob at Bolton, but when he ventured outside, opposition melted. " I called for a chair. The winds were hushed, and all was calm and still. My heart was filled with love, my eyes with tears, and my mouth with arguments. They were amazed ; they were ashamed; they were melted down ; they devoured every word. What a turn was this ! Oh, how did God change the counsel of the old Ahithophel into foolishness, and bring all the drunkards, swearers, Sabbath breakers, and mere sinners in the place to hear of His bounteous redemption ! " Charles Wesley and his companion Mr. Meriton had a terrible experience of the mob at Devizes, in February, 1747. Such diabolical malice Charles Wesley had never before seen. Methodism was indeed cradled amid persecutions of every kind. The Wesleys had to bear the brunt of this opposition, but both preachers and people shared the baptism. There are no pages more exciting, and none more heroic in history than these records of constancy under the fiercest trials.

DISTINCTIVE TEACHING.

Methodist Doctrine.—Wesley was faithful to the distinctive teaching of the Reformation, and of the Church of England. Repentance for sin, justification by faith, holiness of heart and life—these were the doctrines of the Evangelical Revival. The publication of Wesley's sermon on " Free Grace," in 1740, greatly disturbed Whitefield, who had adopted Calvinistic views, and was very anxious that this sermon should not be printed. But the Wesleys did not feel that they could hold their peace when such an issue was at stake. They were daily being brought into contact with sin in every form, and they clearly saw that nothing short of a salvation, by which every soul might be restored to the favour and image of God, would meet the needs of the world. In this convietion they never wavered.

Dr. Dale has shown how different Wesley's Arminianism was from that held by many Nonconformists of the last century. The cold and powerless conception of God, these teachers had drawn from Deism, coloured their theology. Man was free partly because God was far off. Wesley had a nobler and more vital faith. "He believed that in God we live and move and have our being. And yet in the strength of his own moral life, he had a most vivid consciousness that he was morally free—free to receive or reject the infinite grace which the living God was pressing upon him ; and therefore he was an Arminian."

A great deal of bitterness was aroused by the Calvinistic controversy, but the Wesleys never lost their love for Whitefield, and though he preached against them by name and refused to work with them, he grew more reasonable as time went on. In later years, Whitefield took service occasionally in the Methodist chapels, and Wesley preached his friend's funeral sermon at Tottenham Court Road in 1770.

Assurance of Salvation.—Wesley's long struggle with spiritual darkness, led him to lay great stress on the truth that every Christian might enjoy the assurance of acceptance with God. We have seen how hardly he judged himself on his voyage from America, and have noted how he afterwards modified his judgment. The early Methodist preaching was no doubt somewhat extreme in this direction, for Wesley, in referring to it, says : "I wonder the people of England did not stone us." But Wesley and his helpers never failed to teach that salvation was offered to every man, and that all who believed in Christ, might enjoy the witness of their acceptance. Wesley saw clearly that defects of training or teaching, and peculiarities of temperament, might rob some of the joy which they ought to know. He did not unchristianize them for these things as he had been tempted to do in the first ardour of his own religious life, but he sought to lead them into the joy of an experience which would set their hearts at rest, and prepare them for usefulness. The testimony of the Spirit he defined as "an inward impression on the soul, whereby the Spirit of God directly witnesses to my Spirit, that I am a child of God ; that Jesus Christ hath loved me, and given Himself for me ; and that all my sins are blotted out, and I, even I, am reconciled to God' (*Works*, v. 115). That testimony every Christian might enjoy as he himself enjoyed it. Such teaching gave Methodism its vitality. People and preachers felt a spirit of "exhilaration, vigour, triumph. Their joy was irresistible. It broke out in

shouts of Hallelujah. It sung exulting songs." It made
Methodism superior to mobs and persecutions, and nerved it to
continual labour for the salvation of the world.

Entire Sanctification.—Wesley's doctrine of entire sanctification was also one of the distinctive notes of his teaching. He
held that when a man is justified, inward sanctification begins,
and that as he grows in grace the work is carried on till he is
" sanctified throughout in spirit, soul, and body." (*Min.*, 1745.)
Christian perfection he defined as " the humble, gentle, patient
love of God and our neighbour, ruling our tempers, words, and
actions." He did not contend for the term sinless, though he
did not object to it, but he held that Christians were not free
from ignorance, mistake, infirmity or temptation, though they
might be so far perfect as to be delivered from outward sin,
evil thoughts and evil tempers. He believed that the blessing
was wrought in the soul by an act of faith, preceded and
followed by a gradual work of grace. Thomas à Kempis,
Jeremy Taylor, and William Law, first taught him when he
was at Oxford to seek that purity of intention, that entire consecration of body, soul and substance to God, which was the
kernel of his later teaching, and from the position taken at
Oxford he never swerved. His teaching was greatly misunder-
stood; but when he explained it to the Bishop of London, Dr.
Gibson replied : " Mr. Wesley, if this be all you mean, publish
it to all the world. If anyone then can confute what you say,
he may have free leave."

Appeals to Men of Reason and Religion.—Nothing that
Wesley wrote did more to allay prejudice and win the confidence and respect of thoughtful people than his " Appeals to
Men of Reason and Religion." Their dignity and tenderness,
the calm reasonableness, and the manifest sincerity which
breathe throughout them, made a profound impression.
Wesley says : he thought the " Farther Appeal " would have
enraged the world beyond measure, but on the contrary, it
seems nothing was ever published which softened them so
much. The Apologia for Methodism and its leaders in the
opening of the first Appeal is singularly attractive. " We see,
(and who does not ?) the numberless follies and miseries of our
fellow-creatures. We see, on every side, either men of no
religion at all, or men of a lifeless, formal religion. We are
grieved at the sight, and should greatly rejoice, if by any means
we might convince some that there is a better religion to be
attained—a religion worthy of God that gave it. And this we
conceive to be no other than love ; the love of God, and of all
mankind ; the loving God with all our heart, and soul, and
strength, as having first loved *us*, as the fountain of all the
good we have received, and of all we hope to enjoy; and

the loving every soul which God hath made, every man of
earth, as our own soul. This love we believe to be the
medicine of life, the never-failing remedy for all the evils of a
disordered world, for all the miseries and vices of men.
Wherever this is, there are virtue and happiness going hand-in-
hand. There is humbleness of mind, gentleness, long-suffering,
the whole image of God ; and at the same time, a peace that
passeth all understanding, and joy unspeakable and full of glory."

Elements of Success.—After the year 1742, Methodism
began to spread rapidly over England. It was peculiarly
fitted to attract earnest-minded men. Its doctrines of free
grace, personal salvation, and entire sanctification gave it a
message for all the world ; every street and common furnished
a stand for its preachers. It had an organisation singularly
adopted to its purpose. The class meeting conserved and
deepened the results of the preaching, whilst band meetings,
love feasts, watch nights, supplied all the helps that young
Christians, and those also who were more experienced and
mature, required. Just when the work began to spread most
rapidly, his noble band of lay preachers was raised up to assist
Wesley. Nor must we forget the hymnology of the Revival.
Dr. Stoughton says : " Methodism never could have become
what it did without its unparalleled hymn book. That, perhaps,
has been more effective in preserving its evangelical theology,
than Wesley's Sermons and his Notes on the New Testament.
Where one man read the homilies and the exposition, a thousand sang the hymns." Yet with all these combined influences
of psalmody, doctrine, and organisation, Methodism could
never have gained its position had not John Wesley been at its
head. He was entirely consecrated to his work. No personal
ambition touched him. He devoted time, fortune, strength,
refinement, education, and his rare gifts of intellect and heart to
the cause. Macaulay says justly that his genius for organisation, was as great as that of Richelieu, and it was combined
with a power to rise above prejudice, which made him ready to
learn from anyone, an industry that has scarcely any parallel,
and a calm faith in God which rose superior to all difficulties
and discouragements.

SOME MEMORABLE INCIDENTS.

The Wesleys Marry.—Charles Wesley was married to
Miss Sarah Gwynne, the daughter of a Welsh magistrate, on
April 8th, 1749, and settled in Bristol, which became his home
for the next twenty-two years. His strength was henceforth
chiefly given to London and Bristol, but, in 1751, he made an
extended tour over all the Societies as far north as Newcastle.
In 1753, he paid his last visit to Cornwall. "This place seems

quite subdued to our Lord. Their hearts are all bowed before
Him. He gives me uncommon strength. A very great door
is opened." A few months later, John Wesley was threatened
with consumption, and Charles hastened to Lewisham, where
he found his brother prostrate. "It is most probable," he
wrote, "that he will not recover, being far gone in galloping
consumption, just as my elder brother was at his age."
Charles told the Society at the Foundery, that he neither could
nor would stand in his brother's place (if God took him to Himself) ; for he had neither a body, nor a mind, nor tàlents, nor
grace for it. The blow which he feared, did not fall, but it is
manifest that Charles Wesley was quite unfit to take his
brother's place. John Wesley had henceforth to bear the
burden of leadership alone. Meanwhile Methodism was
" widening and deepening, not only in London and Bristol, but
in most parts of England ; there being scarce any county, and
not many large towns, wherein there were not more or fewer
witnesses of it." Wesley was married to Mrs. Vazeille, the
widow of a London merchant, in February, 1751, but the
union proved disastrous. Mrs. Wesley travelled extensively
with her husband during the first four years of her marriage,
but she was a woman of violent and suspicious temper, and
after causing Wesley many sorrows, she left him, never to
return. This domestic trouble was not without compensations.
Had she been a better wife, Wesley feared that regard for her
wishes might have made him unfaithful to his itinerant life.

John Fletcher.—On March 13th, 1757, Wesley was feeling
quite unequal to his heavy Sunday's work, which he considered
equal to preaching eight sermons. As soon as he finished his
discourse at West Street, a young Swiss clergyman who had
been ordained that morning at Whitehall, came in to his aid.
Wesley says : "How wonderful are the ways of God ! When
my bodily strength failed, and no clergyman in England was
able and willing to assist me, He sent me help from the moun-
tains of Switzerland, and a help meet for me in every respect.
Where could I have found such another ? " Fletcher was then
twenty-nine. For eighteen years he was Wesley's chief helper.
Fletcher is the saint of the revival. He had to defend Methodist
teaching against the most virulent assault, but even as a controversialist his Christian temper was as conspicuous as his logical
acumen. He became Vicar of Madeley, in Shropshire, and married
Mary Bosanquet, the elect lady of Methodism. Fletcher, it was
hoped, would eventually take Wesley's place as leader of the
United Societies, but he died in 1775. Isaac Taylor says :
" the Methodism of Fletcher was Christianity, as little lowered
by admixture of human infirmity as we may hope to find it
anywhere on earth."

Calvinistic Controversy.—The year 1770 was an epoch in the history of Methodism. At the Conference, a membership of 29,406 was reported in fifty circuits. There were 121 preachers, and more than 100 chapels. A great effort had been made in 1767 to deal with the chapel debts which stood at £11,383. £8,700 of this was cleared off, but as new chapels were springing up everywhere, it was a serious tax on Wesley's resources. The chief anxiety of the year was caused by the Calvinistic Controversy, which arose through some doctrinal Minutes intended as a guard against the antinomianism which was causing such mischief in Wesley's Societies at Norwich, Manchester, Dublin, and other places. The Countess of Huntingdon had become a strong Calvinist, and broke off her friendship with the Wesleys on account of these Minutes. Years of controversy followed. It is not pleasant to remember the virulent attacks of Toplady and Sir Richard and Rowland Hill, but Fletcher conducted the controversy in a spirit which has won him enduring honour. Whitefield died in America before the painful struggle began.

City Road Chapel.—The head-quarters of Methodism for nearly forty years was the Foundery in Moorfields. This had long been a most inadequate building, and great was the rejoicing when City Road Chapel was opened on November 1st, 1778. It was commodious enough to hold all the London members at the annual Covenant Service. In the preacher's house, on the south side of the Chapel, Wesley lived with his staff of helpers. Here he died, and was buried in the adjoining graveyard. The Prayers of the Church of England were read here both morning and evening by an ordained clergyman, and at first the Wesleys or some other clergyman always occupied the pulpit. Charles Wesley had moved to Marylebone in 1771, so that he was able to give his chief attention to City Road. He would gladly have preached there twice every Sunday, but the trustees and people were naturally anxious that the itinerant preachers should not be excluded from the chief pulpit of Methodism.

The Deed of Declaration.—The Conference did not receive a legal constitution till the year 1784. The trustees of the chapel at Birstall claimed the right to appoint preachers for that chapel after Wesley's death. He saw that this meant the wreck of Methodism, and his firmness finally won the day. This struggle showed the necessity of setting the Connexion on a more sound basis. On February 28th, 1784, Wesley executed the Deed of Declaration. It contained the names of one hundred preachers who were to form the Legal Conference. They were authorized to meet once a year, fill up vacancies in their own number, appoint a President and Secretary, station the preachers, admit proper persons into the Ministry, and take general oversight of the Societies.

American Methodism.—In 1758, Wesley visited the little community of Palatines settled in Limerick. The Methodist preachers had been there before him, and a great work had broken out among the German immigrants. Two years later, a party of them emigrated to America, and became the founders of Methodism in the New World. Barbara Heck roused Philip Embury, who had been a local preacher in Ireland, to hold service in his own house in New York. This was in the Autumn of 1766. Two classes were formed, and next year, a rigging loft was hired for services. On October 30th, 1768, a chapel was opened in John Street, and a pressing call was sent to Wesley for workers. " Send us a preacher" they said, "for the good of thousands, send one at once. With a man whose heart and soul are in the work," they predicted that " such a flame would soon be kindled as would never stop till it reached the great South Sea. When the Conference of 1769 met at Leeds, Wesley asked, " Who is willing to go ? " The answer was "two of our preachers, Richard Boardman, and Joseph Pilmoor, willingly offered themselves for this service ; by whom we determined to send them £50, as a token of our brotherly love, and £20 we gave to our brethren for their passage." Embury had found a grand ally in Captain Webb, then a lieutenant in the 48th regiment, who drew great congregations to the rigging loft and to the chapel. He passed up and down the country preaching, and introduced Methodism into Philadelphia and other places. Robert Strawbridge, another local preacher from Ireland, had settled in Maryland, about 1766, and formed several societies. When Boardman and Pilmoor arrived, the work made rapid strides.

Bishop Asbury.—At the Conference of 1771, Wesley says: "Our brethren in America call aloud for help. Who are willing to go over and help them ? " Richard Wright and Francis Asbury responded to this appeal. Asbury was now about twenty-six. He was the son of a labouring man at Handsworth, and had been five years a Methodist preacher. He became the Wesley of the New World, travelling east and west, north and south, to direct the work of Methodism, which was spreading by leaps and bounds over all the States. The breach between the colonies and the mother country left the Methodists of America in great straits. Wesley at last decided to ordain Coke as Superintendent or Bishop. When he arrived he was to ordain Asbury as his colleague. The Conference met at Baltimore, in December, 1784. Asbury was ordained, and then set apart as Bishop. The Methodist Episcopal Church was thus formed. It had 293 preachers,

45,384 white and 11,280 coloured members. Asbury became the central figure of American Methodism. He preached 16,500 sermons, rode 270,000 miles, presided in not less than 224 Annual Conferences, ordained more than 4,000 preachers. Asbury was a born leader who knew how to choose his men ; his own zeal and enthusiasm never flagged. He continued his travels to the last, even when he had to be helped up the pulpit stairs, and to sit while preaching. When he died in March, 1816, there were 211,000 Methodists in America with more than 700 itinerant preachers. American Methodism in all its branches now has 32,369 Ministers, 53,537 Churches, 5,124,636 communicants. The Roman Catholics have 7,742,774 communicants, the Baptists 3,926,183, the Presbyterians 1,416,204, the Protestant Episcopalians 600,764, the Congregationalists 580,000.

WESLEY'S CHURCHMANSHIP AND WORK.

Wesley's Views on Orders.—Wesley regarded his preachers as laymen, and did not allow them to administer the Sacraments. Such duties belonged to those who held " a commission so to do from those Bishops whom we apprehend to be in a succession from the Apostles." But in the beginning of 1746, three weeks after he had expressed this conviction, Lord King's " Account of the Primitive Church " opened Wesley's eyes. He wrote " In spite of the vehement prejudice of my education, I was ready to believe that this was a fair and impartial draft ; but if so, it would follow that Bishops and Presbyters are (essentially) of one order, and that originally every Christian congregation was a Church independent on all others." Wesley gradually saw that he had as much right to ordain as to administer the Sacraments. In 1784, he told his brother—" I firmly believe I am a Scriptural ἐπίσκοπος as much as any man in England, or in Europe ; for the uninterrupted succession I know to be a fable, which no man ever did or can prove."

Wesley's Ordinations.—Acting on this conviction, Wesley ordained Dr. Coke as Superintendent or Bishop for the American Societies. As soon as Coke reached America he was to set apart Francis Asbury to the same office. Wesley was assisted in Coke's ordination by the Rev. James Creighton, a clergyman who administered the Sacrament to the Methodist Societies in and around London. Wesley, Coke and Creighton, then ordained Richard Whatcoat and Thomas Vasey to administer the Sacraments in America. The Annals of the S.P.G. and Bishop Seabury's life abundantly justify the course Wesley took. The need of a bishop had been keenly felt for eighty years. One of the agents of the S.P.G. wrote in 1716 : "I don't pretend to prophesy, but you know how 'tis said, the kingdom of God shall be taken from them, and given to a

nation that will bring forth the fruits of it. I cannot but think
the honourable Society had done more if they had found *one*
honest man to bring Gospel Orders over to us." Wesley urged
Dr. Lowth, Bishop of London, to ordain someone to minister
to the people, but he pleaded in vain. Even Seabury was
compelled to seek his orders from the Scotch bishops. The
United States were now separated from the mother country.
Most of the English clergy had left their posts, and eighteen
thousand Methodists were without the Sacraments. Asbury
prevailed on the preachers to give up the administration of the
Sacraments, on which some of them had ventured, and urged
Wesley to send them help. It would have been inexcusable to
neglect that call. Wesley therefore took the decisive step and
set apart Coke and his companions for this work. Other
ordinations followed. On August 1st, 1785, Wesley says:
"Having with a few select friends weighed the matter
thoroughly, I yielded to their judgment, and set apart three
of our well-tried preachers—John Pawson, Thomas Hanby,
and Joseph Taylor, to minister in Scotland." At the Conference of 1786, he ordained Joshua Keighley and Charles
Atmore for Scotland, William Warrener for Antigua, William
Hammet for Newfoundland. In 1787, five others were
ordained, and in 1788, when in Scotland, he set apart John
Barber and Joseph Cownley. He also ordained Alexander
Mather, not only as elder, but also as bishop. On Ash Wednesday, 1789, Wesley ordained Henry Moore and Thomas
Rankin, "not for Scotland or America any more than I am,"
Bradburn said, but for England. The same year Wesley
invited his assistant, William Myles, an unordained preacher,
to assist him by giving the cup to the communicants in Dublin.
In taking this course, Wesley had the authority of such men as
Stillingfleet behind him. That learned bishop says, "In the
first Primitive Church the presbyters all acted in common for
the welfare of the Church, and either did, or might, ordain
others to the same authority with themselves, because the
intrinsical power of order is equally in them and in those who
were afterwards appointed governors over presbyters."

Wesley and the Church of England.—Wesley never lost
his love for the Church of England. The Churches were
closed against him, and the clergy often led the mob that tried
to drive out the Methodists, yet Wesley's attachment to the
Church survived all assaults. He hoped that his people would
never leave the Church of England, and even went so far as
to say in 1787: "When the Methodists leave the Church of
England, God will leave them." But whilst this is true,
Wesley took every precaution to secure the continuance of
Methodism. During his last years, though he was treated with

profound respect by the clergy, and invited to fill their pulpits, he ordained Ministers not only for America, but for England. Charles Wesley was greatly distressed, and pleaded with his brother to allow him to go to the grave before the bridge between Methodism and the Church of England was quite broken down. Lord Mansfield, whom Charles consulted, naturally regarded ordination as separation. But circumstances were forcing Wesley's hand. It was easy for Charles Wesley, who had long stood aloof from the general trend of Methodist feeling, and had known little of the Societies outside London and Bristol for thirty years, to speak as he did. In London the Sacrament was administered every week at West Street, and even after Charles Wesley removed from Bristol, arrangements were made that the Lord's Supper should be administered there every other Sunday. But the country Methodists were in an altogether different position. Wesley did his best to hold his members to the Church, but they were often repelled from the Lord's table, and still oftener felt that the character of the clergyman made it impossible to take the Sacrament from his hands with profit.

This was no new difficulty. It was felt so acutely in the year 1755, that Joseph Cownley, whom Wesley regarded as one of his best preachers, Thomas Walsh, the devoted Irish Evangelist, and the two sons of Mr. Perronet, Vicar of Shoreham, whom Charles Wesley called the Archbishop of Methodism, went so far as to absent themselves from the services of the Church, and to administer the Lord's Supper to the people and to each other. John Wesley wrote to his brother that Cownley said : " For such and such reasons I dare not hear a drunkard preach or read prayers. I answer, I dare. But I cannot answer his reasons." The Conference of 1755, which met in Leeds, discussed this question. Sixty-three preachers were present. The Wesleys expressed their views strongly, and then asked whether the preachers thought the Methodists ought to separate from the Church. After a three days' debate, all agreed that whether lawful or not, this was not expedient. Walsh and his friends agreed not to administer the Sacrament. With this decision, John Wesley was content. Charles saw that many of the preachers were unconvinced, and that the evil day was only postponed. He would have compelled every preacher to choose between " the Church and the Meeting." His fears continued, and next month, Wesley wrote " Here is Charles Perronet, raving because his friends have given up all ; and Charles Wesley, because they have given up nothing ; and I, in the midst, staring and wondering both at one and the other."

Respect for Wesley's personal wishes, led the preachers to their decision in 1755, but the difficulty still continued. Wesley

was not blind to the situation.   In 1786, he says that the last
time he visited Scarborough, he earnestly exhorted the
Methodists to go to Church, and went himself.   "But the
wretched Minister preached such a sermon, that I could not in
conscience advise them to hear him any more."   At Epworth,
in July, 1788, there were scarcely twenty communicants, half
of whom had gone on Wesley's account.   He says : " I would
fain prevent the members here from leaving the Church, but I
cannot do it.   As Mr. G. is not a pious man, but rather an enemy
to piety, who frequently preaches against the truth, and those
that hold and love it, I cannot, with all my influence, persuade
them either to hear him, or to attend the Sacrament administered by him.   If I cannot carry this point while I live, who
then can do it when I die ?   And the case of Epworth is the
case of every Church where the Minister neither loves nor
preaches the Gospel.   The Methodists will not attend his
ministrations.   What, then, is to be done?"   The old leader
left the door open for closer fellowship between his Societies
and the Church, had he not done so, he would have been
unfaithful to the convictions of a lifetime, but he secured the
independence of Methodism, and left its Conference with hands
free to follow the leadings of providence.   He must have seen,
despite his affection for the Church of England, that separation
was inevitable, and the provision made in his last years shows
clearly that he prized the continuance of Methodism much more
highly than its connexion with the Church of England.

John Pawson, President of the Conference in 1793, bears
emphatic testimony to this.   He says : Wesley "foresaw that
the Methodists would, after his death, soon become a distinct
people ; he was deeply prejudiced against a Presbyterian, and
was much in favour of an Episcopal form of Government ; in
order, therefore, to preserve all that was valuable in the Church
of England among the Methodists, he ordained Mr. Mather
and Dr. Coke bishops.   These he undoubtedly designed, should
ordain others.   Mr. Mather told us so at the Manchester
Conference ; but we did not then understand him."

John Murlin confirms Mather.   " By the preparation which
Mr. Wesley made before his death, it appears to a demonstra-
tion that he intended there should be a further alteration after
he was dead.   If he did not intend a further alteration, why
did he ordain Dr. Coke and Alexander Mather bishops?   We
can have no doubt, but that he intended that they should
ordain others."

Henry Moore also in a letter to the Conference of 1837,
states that when Mr. Wesley ordained Alexander Mather,
Thomas Rankin, and himself, he did it to provide for the
ordination of all the Methodist preachers if need should arise,

" I am the only person now living that Mr. Wesley committed. that power to, *i.e.* the power to ordain, and I know that he committed it for the purpose that it should become a common thing whenever it should be judged by the Conference best to adopt it."

Appearance and Habits.—John Wesley was not quite five feet six inches high, and weighed eight stone ten pounds. He had a fine forehead, a piercing eye, an aquiline nose, and was scrupulously neat in dress and habits. He was never in a hurry, but never lost a moment. Someone asked how he managed to do so much work in so short a time : " Brother," he replied, " I do only one thing at a time, and I do it with all my might." He was never despondent, did not in fact remember having suffered a quarter of an hour from lowness of spirits in his life. His perfect courtesy and abundant store of anecdote, made him a delightful companion. Young people always loved him. A more unselfish man never lived. As his cheap pub-lications began to yield large profits, he was able to help many who were in need. In later life, he gave away £1,000 a year in charity. He was well aware of his genius for administration. " I know," he said, " this is the peculiar talent which God has given me." Methodism was a kind of providential mosaic, into which one feature after another was fitted with wonderful skill. Wesley had not so much the power of invention as the art of adopting every wise suggestion and weaving it into his system.

Wesley as a Preacher.—Wesley's style was modelled on the First Epistle of St. John, which he considered to be a perfect example of the highest thinking put into the simplest words. " Here," he says, " are sublimity and simplicity together, the strongest sense, and the plainest language ! How can anyone that would 'speak as the oracles of God,' use harder words than are found here?" He learned this art of simplicity early, and had become an extempore preacher before he went to Georgia. For closeness and pungency, there was no preaching of the Evangelical Revival to compare with Wesley's. He made appeals to the heart and conscience which were well-nigh irresistible; and his applications were peculiarly powerful. The sermons which he heard in the Scotch kirks seemed specially defective in this respect. He says of one " As there was no application, it is likely to do as much good as the singing of a lark." Wesley's attitude was graceful, his action calm and natural, his voice so clear that it was once found that it could be distinctly heard a hundred and forty yards away. He was sometimes so much drawn out toward his congregation that he " continued three hours." But these were times of peculiar influence, in days when there was a great hunger for the Gospel message. In his last years he seldom preached for more than half-an-hour.

Cheap Literature.—No man in his century did more for popular literature than Wesley. Himself a great reader, and a man of catholic tastes, he clearly recognised that if Methodism was to keep its hold, it must teach its people to read. There were but few books suitable for his purpose in those days, and their price put them out of the reach of miners, tinners, weavers and peasants. Wesley therefore set himself to supply the need. Mr. Leslie Stephen pays high tribute to his remarkable literary power. He says that he goes straight to the mark without one superfluous flourish. Besides his journals, he published many of his works and his brother's hymns in the form of penny tracts. His sermons, appeals, educational and biographical works, had a wide circulation. When he set up a carriage, he always had a store of books with him, and sometimes spent ten hours alone on his long journeys. He bought up every moment of quiet, that he might provide reading for his people, and found his work so acceptable, that he " unawares became rich.'' He created an appetite for reading among the masses, and, as Methodism spread over the kingdom, the demand for his books became enormous. He had a Tract Society in 1747, and wrote some of the most pungent tracts ever penned. "A Word to a Drunkard," "A Word to a Smuggler," "A Word to a Sabbath-Breaker"—are wonderful for their directness and vigour. A whole battery seems to open on the reader, and he is glad to capitulate without delay.

Wesley as a Social Reformer.—As a Social Reformer, Wesley was far in advance of his time. He found work for the deserving poor, provided them with clothes and food in seasons of special distress, established a lending stock to help struggling business men with loans. He opened dispensaries in London and Bristol, and did everything he could to assist debtors who had been thrown into prison. Some of the most stirring stories of Wesley's life are connected with these labours of love. In his eighty-second year, we see him hastening about the London streets, which were filled with melting snow, to beg money for the poor. Two years later, he made another begging tour of the metropolis, which yielded two hundred pounds for his charities. In visiting the prisons, in temperance work, in care for the debtor, and in opposition to the slave trade Wesley was far in advance of his time. He was a lover of all good work, and a hearty supporter of those who were seeking to redress the crying wrongs of the world.

The Sunday School movement which began to spread in his last years, had his powerful support. " This," he said, " is one of the best institutions which have been seen in Europe for some centuries, and will do more and more good, provided the teachers and inspectors do their duty. Nothing can prevent the success of this blessed work, but the neglect of the instruments." His delight in the Sunday Scholars, at Bolton, in 1788, and in their singing—" I defy any to exceed it; except the singing of angels in our Father's house "—must have filled Methodism with new interest in this growing institution. Miss Hannah Ball, of High Wycombe, who began a Sunday School there in 1769, fourteen years before Raikes started his at Gloucester, was one of Wesley's members, and sent him details of her effort for her "wild little company."

Charles Wesley's Death.—Charles Wesley died at his house in Marylebone, on March 29th, 1788. In his last years, he had given much of his strength to the prisoners at Newgate. The love for the outcast, which had led him to such blessed work at Oxford and London at the beginning of the Revival, still burned brightly in the old man's heart. He was surrounded by a noble group of friends. Lord Mansfield, who had been his schoolfellow at Westminster, often walked over from Bloomsbury Square to visit him. The Earl of Dartmouth, Lord Mornington (the father of the Duke of Wellington), Dr. Johnson, William Wilberforce, and Hannah More, were firmly attached to the Poet of Methodism. His muse was busy to the last. On his death bed, he called his wife, and asked her to write down his latest verse :

> In age and feebleness extreme,
> Who shall a sinful worm redeem?
> Jesus ! my only hope Thou art,
> Strength of my failing flesh and heart;
> Oh, could I catch one smile from Thee,
> And drop into eternity !

Charles Wesley rests in the peaceful little graveyard of Marylebone old Parish Church. John was in Shropshire when his brother died, and through the delay of a letter, was not able to return in time for the funeral, but he proved a true counsellor and friend to the widow and her three gifted children. Charles Wesley wrote no less than 6,500 hymns. The deepest experiences of his own heart are revealed in his verse, and every phase of the Great Revival seems mirrored there for all time. He has been pronounced to be " the great hymn writer of all ages." For half a century his muse was consecrated to the Evangelical Revival. " In his hymns the vast congregations that gathered in the churchyards, on the hill-side, at the market-cross, or in the streets of town or cities throughout the kingdom, found expression for their conviction of sin and yearning after mercy. Here, too, when the burden of guilt and dread rolled away, their full hearts found a voice. His hymns added another application to many a powerful sermon, and lingered with the hearers long after the itinerant preachers had hurried on to another congregation."

John Wesley's Last Years and Death.—John Wesley lived three years after his brother Charles. He was still as full of zeal as in the early days of the Revival, and though his infirmities were increasing, he never paused in his itinerancy. The Methodists felt that he could not long be with them, and hung upon his lips wherever he went. Persecution and reproach had long since ceased. Wesley was the best loved, and most popular man in England. People gazed on the old veteran with veneration as he passed along the streets, and flocked in crowds to hear his message. His constant prayer was "Lord, let me not live to be useless!" He generally closed his counsels to the Society with the lines:

> Oh that without a lingering groan
>   I may the welcome word receive!
> My body with my charge lay down,
>   And cease at once to work and live.

He preached his last open-air sermon, at Winchelsea, on October 6th, 1790, and his last sermon at Leatherhead, on February 22nd, 1791, from the words: "Seek ye the Lord while He may be found; call ye upon Him while He is near." His last letter written to William Wilberforce, bearing date February 24th, bade the champion of liberty "go on, in the name of God, and in the power of His might, till even American slavery, the vilest that ever saw the sun, shall vanish away before it." The old veteran died at his house in City Road, on Wednesday, March 2nd, 1791, in the eighty-eighth year of his age. During the last night of his life, he was heard to whisper "I'll praise, I'll praise." A more beautiful death-bed scene is scarcely to be found in history than John Wesley's. As he passed within the veil, his friends standing round the bed, sang

> Waiting to receive thy spirit,
>   Lo! the Saviour stands above;
> Shows the purchase of His merit,
>   Reaches out the crown of love.

As many as ten thousand people came to look on him as he lay in City Road Chapel, on the day before his burial. He rests in the graveyard behind his Cathedral Church, with those memorable words on his tombstone: "Reader, if thou art constrained to bless the instrument, give God the Glory."

Wesley's Sayings.—Some glimpses into Wesley's mind and heart may be gained by gathering together a few of his best known sayings. At Oxford he formed his great resolve. "Leisure and I have taken leave of one another. I propose to be busy as long as I live, if my health is so long indulged me." In 1739, when the field-preaching began, he wrote: "I look upon all the world as my parish; thus far I mean, that, in whatever part of it I am, I judge it meet, right, and my bounden duty, to declare unto all that are willing to hear, the glad tidings of salvation." When he prepared his printed sermons, he thus expressed his longing for guidance. "I want to know one thing, the way to heaven, how to land safe on that happy shore. God Himself has condescended to teach me the way; for this very end He came down from heaven. He hath written it down in a book. Oh, give me that book! At any price, give me the book of God! I have it; here is knowledge enough for me. Let me be *homo unius libri*." He gloried in the peace which true religion brought in life's darkest hours: "The world may not like our Methodists and Evangelical people, but the world cannot deny that they die well." His manner of work is thus expressed, "Though I am always in haste, I am never in a hurry, because I never undertake any more work than I can get through with perfect calmness of spirit." His quiet trust in God breathes in the words: "By the grace of God, I never fret; I repine at nothing; I am discontented with nothing. I see God sitting upon His throne, and ruling all things well." His death-bed sayings will never cease to be cherished in Methodism: "How necessary it is for everyone to be on the right foundation!

> I the chief of sinners am,
> But Jesus died for me.

We must be justified by faith, and then go on to full perfection." This confidence was his only hope in the presence of eternity. His legacy to Methodism was that burst of exulting faith, "The best of all is, God is with us." In this assurance his first followers faced the trials that followed his departure from their midst. It is still the watchword of Methodism.

CHAPTER III.

METHODISM SINCE WESLEY'S DEATH.

SACRAMENTAL CONTROVERSY, ETC.

Arrangements after Wesley's Death.—Wesley died on March 2nd, 1791. The same day, a printed letter signed by the London preachers, was sent to their brethren in the country. It ran thus: "The melancholy period we have so long dreaded, is now arrived.—Our aged and honoured father, Mr. Wesley, is no more! He was taken to Paradise this morning, in a glorious manner, after a sickness of five days. We have not time to say more at present relative to his demise.—Only what respects our future economy. This injunction he laid upon us, and all our brethren on his death-bed, that we each continue in our respective station till the time appointed for the next Conference at Manchester. We have, therefore, no doubt but you will, with us, readily comply with his dying request. The more so, as this is consonant with the determination of the Conference held at Bristol, when he was supposed to be near death there, and confirmed in succeeding Conferences."

The day before Wesley's funeral, a "short, but authentic narrative" of his last hours, drawn up by Miss Ritchie, was sent to friends in the country, who were anxious for particulars of the closing scene. The gravity of the outlook for the United Societies is marked by the postscript. "N.B.—It is judged necessary by the preachers in London, and earnestly recommended to their Brethren, the Preachers and the Societies in their respective Circuits, that in consideration of our late great loss, Wednesday, the 6th of April, be kept as a day of solemn fasting and prayer, in order to humble ourselves before the Lord, and implore the continuance of his mercies towards us. It is also judged needful that Friday, the 1st of July, be kept as another day of solemn fasting and prayer for all the Methodist Societies, in order to implore the blessing of God on the ensuing Conference."

Parties in Methodism.—Methodism at the death of its Founder, was divided into three parties. The large proportion of its members had been gathered out of the world by the labours of Wesley and his preachers. They had few links either to the Church of England, or Dissent, but naturally expected to find all the means of grace where they had found personal salvation. They had been taught to reverence the Sacraments, but were left without any adequate provision for their administration. For many reasons, they desired to have them in their own chapels. On one flank of this central body was the Church party, who wished Methodism to be closely linked to the Church of England, of which they were devoted adherents; on the other flank, was the small, but resolute party of Methodists who leaned to Dissent. The struggle between these conflicting tendencies soon began. Wesley died in troublous times. Europe and America were convulsed by the French Revolution. Burke's "Reflections" and Payne's "Rights of Man," still bear witness to the excitement and unrest which reigned throughout the world. Methodist circles were naturally stirred by the spirit of the times. This must be kept in view as we trace the history of the next few years.

After Wesley's death, meetings of the preachers were held in various parts of the country, to devise means for the preservation of Methodism. Nor were the laymen idle. Eighteen of them met at Hull, on May 4th, to protest against any further deviation from the Church of England, and especially against the administration of the Sacraments in Methodist chapels. Alexander Kilham, one of the younger preachers, prepared a trenchant reply to the circular which they issued. This reply formed a rallying point for those who were opposed to the Hull resolutions. Before the Conference met at Manchester, on July 26th, 1791, Methodism had been inundated by circulars and pamphlets.

Wesley's Letter to the Conference.—Joseph Bradford, Wesley's faithful companion in travel, who had watched over him with such tender care in hours of sickness, delivered a letter to the President, at Manchester, containing Wesley's last counsels to the Conference. It was dated Chester, April 7th, 1785. He said that some of the travelling preachers had expressed a fear lest those who were named in the Deed of Declaration should exclude their brethren " either from preaching in connexion with you, or from some other privileges which they now enjoy. I know no other way to prevent any such inconvenience, than to leave these my last words with you. I beseech you, by the mercies of God, that you never avail yourselves of the Deed of Declaration to assume any superiority over your brethren, but let all things go on among those itinerants who choose to remain together, exactly in the same manner as when I was with you, so far as circumstances will permit. In particular, I beseech you, if you ever loved me, and if you now love God and your brethren, to have no respect for persons in stationing the preachers, in choosing children for the Kingswood school, in disposing of the Yearly Contribution, and the Preachers' Fund, or any other public money. But do all things with a single eye, as I have done from the beginning. Go on thus, doing all things without prejudice or partiality, and God will be with you even to the end." This letter seemed like a voice from heaven. The Conference at once swept away all jealousies by a unanimous resolution, according every privilege conferred by the Deed of Declaration to all preachers in Full Connexion.

The Old Plan and the New.—The relation of the Methodist Societies to the Church of England, and the question of the administration of the Sacrament, caused much anxious thought at this Conference. Those who were attached to the Old Plan, viz. :—a *strict* connexion with the National Church, had printed circular letters strongly insisting that such a course should be adopted. These provoked replies from those who wished the plan to be extended so as to include every *Scriptural* privilege. The Conference of 1791, after due deliberation, resolved, "We engage to follow strictly the plan which Mr. Wesley left us." The Conference could not be more explicit, for it was impossible at this time, to satisfy the contending parties. But the minute was interpreted by each side in the light of its own prepossessions. The Church party maintained that it forbade the administration of the Sacraments save where they had been already granted. Those who were bent on having the Sacraments held that the "old plan had been to follow the openings of Providence," and to amend their plan, as seen needful, in order to be more useful. John Pawson and many eminent preachers and laymen took this view.

The Conference of 1792, which met in London, found that the uneasiness respecting the Sacraments, had increased. Mr. Wesley had been accustomed to administer them on his annual visits to the Societies, and the loss of this privilege, naturally formed a strong argument for the more liberal view. The preachers were themselves divided in opinion. The majority, were, at first, opposed to the innovation, and only yielded when they found how strong the wishes of the people had become a year later. Petitions and addresses from both sides poured in. The Conference, therefore, resolved to decide the question for that year by lot. The verdict was that the Sacraments should not be administered that year. In this odd way, time for fuller reflection was gained. An address was sent to the Societies, explaining the decision, and urging them, despite all difference of sentiments, to live in peace and brotherly love.

Opinion now ripened quickly, and the Leeds Conference of 1793, yielding to the wishes of the people, resolved by a very large majority, that "The Societies should have the privilege of the Lord's Supper, where they unanimously desired it." Many of the Societies availed themselves of this privilege, others quietly went on in the old path. In some places, considerable uneasiness was still felt. The whole question was again discussed in the Bristol Conference of 1794. The Sacrament was finally granted to ninety-three places, the names of which were printed in the Minutes. Conference had scarcely closed before the trustees of Broadmead Chapel, who were much opposed to the administration of the Lord's Supper by the preachers, forbade Henry Moore, who had just been appointed to the Circuit to occupy that pulpit. This brought matters to a crisis. Moore was not the man to give way, and nearly the whole Society withdrew from the chapel from which their preacher had been excluded.

Plan of Pacification.—The Conference of 1795, had to deal with this serious controversy. After a day of fasting and prayer, a committee of nine preachers was appointed to draw up a Plan of Pacification. This was approved, both by the Conference, and by an assembly of trustees, and was cordially received by the Societies. It thus brought to a happy close the four years' struggle as to the Sacraments. In Ireland, a body of "Primitive Wesleyans," separated from the Wesleyan Methodists in 1816, when it was resolved to have the Sacraments in Methodist Chapels, but in 1878, this little body rejoined the Wesleyans.

The Plan of Pacification decreed that the Lord's Supper, Baptism, Burial of the Dead, and Service in Church hours, must not be permitted unless the majority of the trustees, stewards and leaders of a Chapel approved of such a step, and could assure the Conference, in writing, that no separation was likely to be caused. The consent of Conference must be gained before any change was made. Where the Lord's Supper had already been peaceably administered, it was not to be interfered with. The Plan of Pacification also made certain regulations as to the trial of preachers, carefully guarding, however, the sole right of the Conference to appoint the preachers.

In the provisions made as to the Sacraments, Methodism was true to the spirit of its Founder. Wesley always subordinated his own views to the necessities of the work. John Murlin, one of the three preachers who ventured to administer the Lord's Supper at Norwich in 1760, wrote to Joseph Benson, on December 23rd, 1794. " In the infant state of Methodism, the preachers only preached, and did not administer the Sacrament; but near thirty-six years since, Mr. Wesley sent me to Norwich, where I baptised their children, and administered the Lord's Supper, for a great part of three years : as also did others who followed me ; till Mr. Charles made a great outcry, and put a stop to it for a time. Poor man, he was greatly distressed, fearing we were going to invade the Priesthood !" The three preachers acted thus without consultation with the Wesleys. They had taken out licences as Methodist preachers were often compelled to do in self-defence. It was a time of much unrest among the preachers, who found themselves in a trying position between the Church and Dissent. All these difficulties were evidently accentuated at Norwich, which enjoyed an unenviable notoriety in those days for turbulence and heresy. Wesley evidently regarded the action of the preachers and society there as exceptional, and was careful not to interfere hastily.

Further Liberal Measures.—In 1796, Alexander Kilham was expelled from the ranks of the preachers. He had accused his brethren of priestcraft, traduced their characters, and charged them with holding the people in bondage. He used every art to foment discord, and caused considerable disturbance in many of the Societies; but Methodism was scarcely injured at all by the agitation. The New Connexion reported 5,037 members at its first Conference in 1798, but the Wesleyan Connexion continued to show steady increase in numbers. The Conference of 1797 determined to do everything that lay in its power to remove suspicion, and enlist the sympathy and help of the Societies. It was agreed to publish Annual Accounts of the Yearly Collection, and of the school for preachers' sons at Kingswood. All charges for the support of the preachers, were to be laid before their Circuit Quarterly Meeting for approval. The Leaders' Meeting gained a right of veto as to the admission of members, and no one could be expelled till the charges brought against him had been proved before the same meeting. Stewards and Leaders had to be appointed in connection with a Leaders' Meeting; local preachers to be approved by a local preachers' meeting. The Conference maintained its right to appoint preachers, but gave the trustees power to remove any man who was manifestly unfit for his post.

The six years of anxious debate which followed Wesley's death, thus gave to Methodism the shape which it retained till the year 1878, when lay representatives were admitted to Conference. The powers of the trustees were greatly extended, whilst any interference with the rights of Conference was guarded. The Leaders' Meeting took its place as the judicial court of the Society, and its powers were largely increased. The Local Preachers' Meeting gained a definite status, and a large increase of power and responsibility was given to the Circuit Quarterly Meeting. The Conference succeeded to Wesley's rights in fixing the appointments of the preachers, and became the final Court of Appeal in all matters affecting the Societies. In case of new legislation for the Societies at large, power was given to a Quarterly Meeting to suspend its operation in that Circuit till the following Conference. If then confirmed, the rule was binding throughout the Connexion.

Formation of Districts.—To supply the lack of Wesley's personal supervision of the Societies, the Circuits were in 1791, grouped into districts, containing not less than three or more than eight Circuits. England had eighteen Districts, Ireland six, Scotland two, Wales one. The Conference of 1812, directed that the President should always be Chairman of the District in which he was stationed. The Districts had authority to try and suspend any preacher, to deal with Chapel affairs, and with the support of the preachers and their families in each Circuit. They had to select one representative to attend the Stationing Committee, which met before Conference to fix the appointments of the preachers for the year. The Chairman of each District, in conjunction with his brethren in that District

Committee, was responsible to the Conference for the execution of Conference legislation in his District.

Status of the Preachers.—After Wesley's death, when the struggle as to the Sacraments was going on, some of the preachers who had been ordained by Wesley or other clergymen, united in ordaining their brethren. Three were thus set apart at the Newcastle District Meeting, and three at Manchester. The Conference of 1793, resolved that none of the preachers should wear gowns, cassocks, bands or surplices, that the title of Reverend should not be applied to them, and that the distinction between ordained and unordained preachers should be dropped. Twenty years of wonderful growth, made it almost imperative that the preachers of Methodism should have a recognised status. Jabez Bunting, who was rapidly becoming the most influential man in the Connexion, led the way in this matter. It had been usual for the preachers' names to be read out in the Local Preachers' Meeting when examination was made as to character. He objected to have his name thus read, since this was done in its proper place at the District Meeting and the Conference. The matter was brought before Conference, and in the Minutes of 1818 " Rev." is prefixed to the names of all preachers who were members of the Missionary Committee. Bunting struggled hard to persuade the Conference to set apart the young Ministers by imposition of hands, but he failed to carry his brethren with him, and it was not till 1836, that this Scriptural custom was introduced. There were only two dissentients. This form of ordination has ever since been followed in Methodism.

METHODIST MISSIONS.

The Missionary Bishop of Methodism.—In William Carey's " Enquiry into the Obligations of Christians, to Use Means for the Conversion of the Heathens," which was published in 1792, he says, " The late Mr. Wesley made an effort in the West Indies, and some of their ministers are now labouring among the Caribs and negroes, and I have seen pleasing accounts of their success." This sentence shows that Wesleyan Missions are considerably older than the Wesleyan Missionary Society. Dr. Coke is the real father of our Missions. This clergyman had thrown in his lot with Wesley in 1777. In 1784 when he was made the American bishop of Wesley's Societies, he issued " A plan of the Society for the establishment of missions among the heathen." He had set his heart on a mission to the British dominions in Asia, but so many doors were opening nearer home, that he says in 1786 Mr. Wesley felt it imprudent to prosecute this scheme " when so large a field of action is afforded us in countries to which we have so much easier admittance, and where the success, through the blessing of God, is more or less certain."

In 1786 Dr. Coke reports that eleven hundred negroes were members of the Methodist Society in Antigua. He himself visited them before the year was out, and saw what great opportunities there were of usefulness. When he returned to England he begged subscriptions from door to door. Funds were thus provided to send out preachers to Newfoundland and the West Indies. In 1789 a kind of missionary board was formed, consisting of Coke, Mather, Rankin, Rogers, Moore, and Clarke, with three missionary members—Baxter, Warrener and Lumby. Coke was still the missionary collector, who bore the burden of raising funds. After Wesley's death he gave himself to this work in a new spirit of consecration. The Conference of 1791 appointed him their delegate to the West Indies, and formed a committee of nine to examine the missionaries sent out there, and the accounts and letters of the missions. Two years later the first collection was made throughout Methodism for missions. The second was in 1796, and from that time there has been an annual collection. In 1794 Coke published the accounts of the missions from August 1787 to August 1793, showing that he had himself contributed £917 17s. 2¼d., and that £1,250 was due to him from chapels in the West Indies. Since 1804 annual accounts have been published. Dr. Coke was fully recognised as the missionary agent of the Conference in 1799. He was appointed Missionary Treasurer, and had general oversight. In 1803 when Coke was absent in America, the London preachers, with some of the leading laymen, formed themselves into a committee of finance and advice. Mr. Marriott and Mr. Butterworth, the two most eminent London laymen, were appointed treasurer and secretary. The Conference of 1804 named a standing committee, of which Coke was president. No laymen were appointed on it. Its treasurer and secretary were both ministers.

In July, 1813, Coke stood in the Conference at Liverpool pleading for Ceylon. He had said to Adam Clarke a month before, " I am now dead to Europe, and alive for India. God himself has said to me, ' Go to Ceylon!' I am so fully convinced of the will of God, that methinks I had rather be set naked on the coast of Ceylon, without clothes and without a friend, than not go there." The burdens of the Connexion made its wisest counsellors hesitate. The debate was adjourned and Coke spent the night in prayer. Next morning his speech in the Conference, and his offer of £6,000 to begin the mission, overcame all doubt. It was the triumph of his life. His project was sanctioned, and he was empowered to take with him six missionaries. He sailed on December 30th, but next May when the vessel had reached the Indian Ocean, he was found lying lifeless on the floor of his cabin.

Branch Missionary Societies.—Coke kindled a fire which • has never since gone out. Before he left England, the work he loved took new shape. Leeds led the way by forming a Branch Missionary Society in the month of October. Jábez Bunting wrote that they were likely to raise more every year than the doctor had secured by his " occasional applications once in two or three years." The subject of missions, as we have seen, received much anxious consideration at the Conference of 1813. All wished to send the Gospel to the East, but " many were discouraged and some absolutely terrified at the proposal to undertake this work, when funds were so low. But it was at last agreed to diminish the number of preachers at home, in order that we might be enabled, by our frugal savings, to maintain a greater number of missionaries in foreign countries." George Morley, who thus describes the heroic resolve of his brethren, returned to Leeds with a strong determination to make some extraordinary effort for missions. Arrangements were soon made for the first Missionary Meeting. It proved an immediate success. Coke wrote " This blessed plan will lighten my heart exceedingly, both at sea and in Asia." Missionary Societies sprung up all over the country, and the foreign work was set on a solid basis of popular support. The news of Coke's death was a great shock to Methodism. Preachers and people had, with much fear and trembling, yielded to his enthusiasm, and pledged themselves to the Mission in the East. Now the moving mind and heart were gone. Yet Coke's death in the end proved a mighty means of enlisting sympathy and winning resources. Methodism was consecrated afresh to the cause for which her great missionary bishop had lived and died. In 1817 the laws and regulations for the general Missionary Society were adopted by Conference, and the Society was firmly established. The income for the first year was £20,331.

Methodism in Antigua.—Before Coke's departure for Ceylon, the missionary operations of Methodism were confined almost exclusively to the New World. It had been led to occupy these fields by godly laymen, such as Mr. Nathaniel Gilbert, speaker of the House of Assembly in Antigua, whom Wesley visited at Wandsworth, in January, 1758. On his return to Antigua, Mr. Gilbert held Methodist services in his house, which were greatly blessed. After his death two negro slaves kept the society together until in 1778 John Baxter, a Methodist local preacher, came to the island. Coke's visit in 1786 put the work on a new footing, and from that time Methodism in Antigua has had a history of steady progress.

In 1784 preachers were sent to Nova Scotia, where a good work had begun under some English emigrants. The West Indies, Nova Scotia and Newfoundland appear on the Minutes of Conference for the first time in 1785.

Other Missions Founded. — Dr. Coke's interest had been enlisted on behalf of the wandering Foolas, near Sierra Leone, and a little company of mechanics, with a surgeon at their head, had been sent out to teach the natives, but this experiment failed. Sierra Leone had 233 members in 1791, but it was not till 1811 that the Rev. George Warren and three school teachers were sent out. Mr. Warren died in 1812, the first of a long succession of victims to the climate of the West Coast. France appears for the first time in the Minutes of 1816, Spain in 1823, Malta in 1824, Italy in 1860.

Coke's band of missionaries began our flourishing work in Ceylon. In 1817 a mission was formed in Madras, the first of a great series of stations in India. The Rev. John M'Kenny, the first missionary to South Africa, landed at Cape Town in August, 1814. The following August the Rev. Samuel Leigh arrived at Sydney, our first missionary to Australasia. He introduced Methodism to New Zealand in 1818. Success in Australia emboldened the Missionary Committee to send two men to the Friendly Islands in 1826, where multitudes were brought to Christ. In one year 4,000 were added to the Society in Tonga and the neighbouring island. The first assault was made on cannibal Fiji, in 1835, with results which are the chief glory of Methodist missions. A more saintly man than John Hunt, the modern age of Methodism has not produced. He died in 1848, praying with his last breath, " Lord, for Christ's sake, bless Fiji, save Fiji." Amid horrors that baffle description, the English missionaries and their wives toiled on till the whole group of islands was won for Christ. We now have about 3,100 native preachers under the care of nine white missionaries. There are more than 1,322 chapels, 43,339 members and catechumens, 42,807 scholars. Fiji is practically a nation of Methodists. Mr. Piercy, our first worker in China, landed at Hong Kong in 1851. The Burma mission was started in 1887. Ever since Mr. M'Kenny was sent to Cape Town in 1814, Wesleyan missionaries have been at work among the English settlers and the native tribes of Africa. There are flourshing stations in the Transvaal, Swaziland, British Bechuanaland, Mashonaland and Rhodesia. The deadly posts on the West Coast of Africa have never lacked volunteers, and Kumasi has been reoccupied with encouraging promise of success. There is also a hopeful work in Honduras. Besides the large sums provided for missions from the Centenary and Thanksgiving

Funds, the Society's Jubilee Celebration in 1863-1868 yielded £179,000 for foreign work. One of the most useful developments of the past few years is the Foreign Missions Club, with its head quarters in Highbury, and its branch in City Road. The income of the Missionary Society for 1895 was £123,757 and the membership 52,068.

Affiliated Conferences.—A marked feature of Methodist policy has been the formation of affiliated Conferences. Wesley himself not only had his English Conference, but often met his Irish preachers in Conference, and delighted in their unanimity and devotion. The Irish Conference is now held yearly, and is presided over by the President of the English Conference, or some other Minister appointed by that Conference.

We have seen how Wesley laid the basis of the American Conference in 1784. An Upper Canada Conference was formed in 1834, and the missions in Eastern Canada were transferred to it in 1853. The various Methodist bodies in the Dominion were amalgamated into one great Canadian Methodist Church in 1883. The first French Conference met at Nismes in 1852. Three years later the Conference of Eastern British America was formed, including Nova Scotia and Newfoundland. In January, 1855 the first Australian Conference met in Sydney. The missions in New Zealand, Fiji and the Friendly Islands are now under its care. South Africa took Conference rank in 1882, and two West Indian Conferences were formed in 1884. This policy of developing local resources is bearing fruit all round the world.

NOTABLE EVENTS.

Training of Ministers.—Wesley asked in his first Conference, held in 1744, "Can we have a seminary for labourers?" The answer was, "If God spare us to another Conference." Next year the subject was again broached, with the reply, "Not till God give us a proper tutor." Wesley never saw his way to meet this need, but he did his utmost to supply the lack, by gathering his preachers together, and giving them lectures, and also by providing them with suitable books. He urged them to spend, at least, five hours a day in the most useful reading, and told them they must contract a taste for this, or return to their old occupations. "I will give each of you," he promised, "as fast as you will read them, books to the value of five pounds." Adam Clarke, and at least two other preachers had some slight training at Kingswood, but it was not till the Conference of 1834 that a Theological Institution, for the training of ministers was established. Its first home was at Hoxton, but the Centenary

Fund provided for two Colleges at Richmond and Didsbury. Didsbury College was opened on September 22nd, 1842 ; Richmond on September 15th, 1843 ; Headingley, near Leeds, on September 25th, 1868 ; whilst Handsworth, the Birmingham branch, owed its existence to the Thanksgiving Fund of 1878.

Days of Agitation.—Dr. Warren's expulsion from the Methodist Ministry is closely connected with the Institution question. It seems almost certain that disappointed ambition led him to oppose a scheme of which he had long been a most earnest advocate. When Dr. Bunting's name was proposed as President of the Institution, and he found no niche for himself as tutor, Dr. Warren began to veer round. He became a stout opponent of the Institution, and after the decision of the Conference in favour of the scheme, published the speech which he had delivered there with comments manifestly intended to arouse angry feeling in the Methodist Societies, and awaken general opposition to the new project. For this offence he was tried by a Special District Meeting, and suspended from his office as Superintendent. He appealed to the Vice-chancellor's Court, but the action of the District Meeting was upheld, and at the following Conference Dr. Warren was expelled from the Methodist Ministry. He joined the agitators who had been glad to make him their tool, but afterwards retired from their ranks and became a clergyman in Manchester. The consent of the Conference in 1828 to the erection of an organ in Brunswick Chapel, Leeds, had led to a violent agitation, and the formation of a small body of "Protestant Methodists." These now joined Dr. Warren's supporters, the "Wesleyan Methodist Association." The new secession scarcely checked for a moment the progress of the parent body. The political unrest of the times, which formed an important factor in the agitation led by Mr. Kilham, will account largely for the two secessions of 1828 and 1836. More serious trouble followed in 1849. Anonymous papers, called "Fly-sheets," had been circulated among Methodist preachers and people, filled with grievous slanders against the leaders of Methodism and the Conference itself. For their share in this matter James Everett, Samuel Dunn, and William Griffith were expelled from the Ministry. The attack which followed in the press and on the platform was almost incredibly violent and painful. Methodism had a series of decreases which robbed her of 100,000 members, and it was not till 1856 that she begun to recover from the effects of this disastrous agitation. In 1857 the reformers of 1828 and 1836 joined those of 1850 in forming "The Methodist Free Churches."

Primitive Methodists and Bible Christians. — The Primitive Methodist Connexion, which has now gained such a powerful position in many parts of the country, originated in a series of camp meetings, held by Hugh Bourne, a zealous Wesleyan in the Potteries.   He was supported by a local preacher called William Clowes, and on March 14th, 1810, a little Society of ten members was formed, which was the germ of this vigorous Connexion.   It has 4,725 chapels valued at £3,620,000, which provide accommodation for a million people.

The Bible Christians, who closely resemble the Primitive Methodists in character and spirit, have also done good work in the evangelisation of England and the Colonies. The Connexion was founded by a Cornish local preacher called William O'Bryan.   Their first Quarterly Meeting was held at Holsworthy, on January 1st, 1816, when a membership of 237 was reported.   Three years later the first Conference met.   The Bible Christians are specially strong in Cornwall, and Cornish emigrants have propagated this denomination widely in the colonies.

The Centenary of Methodism.—Methodism kept its Centenary in 1839, one hundred years after the first Society had been formed at the Foundery.   At the Inaugural meeting held in Manchester, in October, 1838, noble testimony was borne to the blessing brought by Methodism, and £30,000 was subscribed towards the Centenary Fund.   The first list, published within a fortnight, reached a total of £45,000. Meetings were held all over the country, and £221,939 was subscribed.   £71,609 was devoted to the Theological Institution, £70,000 to the Missionary Society, including £30,000 spent on the Centenary Hall, which furnished much needed offices for the Missionary Society and for Connexional purposes, £38,000 formed a fund for relieving chapels of debt, £16,264 was given for worn-out ministers and their widows, Ireland received £13,415, and the Education Fund £5,051 for the extension of day schools.

Methodism in the Army.—Some of the brightest pages in early Methodist history describe its influence on soldiers. John Haime enlisted in the Queen's Regiment of Dragoons in 1739, and passed through all the perils of the campaign in the Low Countries.   He was under fire for seven hours at Dettingen and seemed to bear a charmed life at Fontenoy. " The hotter the battle grew, the more strength was given me : I was as full of joy as I could contain."   Haime had heard Charles Wesley preach at Brentford before his regiment sailed for Flanders, and told him his state of mind after the service. That conversation was a blessing to him for several years. On the Continent he became a lay preacher.   He sometimes walked twenty and thirty miles a day, and preached thirty-five times a week.   Six other soldiers became preachers, and three hundred men joined the Methodist Society.   At Fontenoy four preachers and many members fell on the field. The courage of the Methodists, and the joy with which they faced death, made a profound impression on their comrades and officers. The Duke of Cumberland had a long conversation with Haime, and heard him preach. He gave orders that he should preach anywhere, and that no one should molest him. Six months after Fontenoy, Charles Wesley's journal describes a little soldiers' dinner party. "We had twenty of our brethren from Flanders to dine with us at the Foundery." Some dragoons of Haime's regiment formed Societies at Dunbar and Musselborough, where they were much blessed to the townsfolk. Eight years after they returned to England, Wesley found eighteen of Haime's dragoons in Society at Manchester, "patterns of seriousness, zeal, and all holy conversation." In Ireland soldiers proved some of the best and bravest of the Methodist converts, and both in Dublin and Cork did much to check the mob and protect the Wesleys and their preachers.

Army Work at Gibraltar.—In 1792 three regiments from Ireland reached Gibraltar. There were a few Methodists among them, and the services which they held attracted so many soldiers and civilians, that next year our Society had one hundred and twenty members. In 1803, two corporals were degraded, and received two hundred lashes each for attending Methodist services. This atrocious sentence, and the severe measures that followed scattered the Society, so that when the Rev. James M'Mullen landed here in 1804, he found only twelve civilians in the Society. He preached once, and then fell a victim with his wife to the yellow fever which was raging. His little daughter, who was brought up under the care of Dr. Adam Clarke, afterwards married the Rev. John Rigg, and became the mother of Dr. Rigg. Four years after Mr. M'Mullen's death another chaplain was sent out. Gibraltar was now the chief home of Methodism in the army. Dr. Rule's appointment as chaplain in 1832 marks the beginning of better days. In 1839, an order was issued by General Lord Hill, Commander-in-chief, which gave every soldier full liberty to attend his own church. It was one thing to secure such an order, and another to get it put into practice. Dr. Rule, however, seemed born to triumph over opposition. When the camp was formed at Aldershot he exerted all his influence to secure due provision for Methodist soldiers. An iron church was built, and through the efforts of Dr. Rule and the Rev. Charles H. Kelly, in June, 1862, after many delays, and not a little opposition, the Wesleyan chaplains won recognition from the War Office, and our work was put on a satisfactory basis. There are now more than 22,000 declared Wesleyans in the Army and Navy, of whom 1,480 are Church members. 195 ministers are wholly or in part devoted to the care of our soldiers and sailors at home and abroad. We have 28 Homes for the men, which have cost £33,797. These provide 432 beds, and are a centre of vigorous social and religious work. They are growing more popular every day. At Aldershot the average number of soldiers attending parade service is nearly 400. The chaplain at Portsmouth has more than 1,000 sailors under his care. No work is bearing better fruit for our empire than this Methodist work in the Army and Navy.

THE METHODISM OF OUR OWN TIMES.

Changes in Conference and District Meeting.— Until the year 1878 the Conference was an assembly of pastors. The Conference of 1801 gave circuit stewards a right to attend the District Meetings and advise in financial matters. In 1803 a Committee was appointed to "guard our religious privileges in these perilous times." Mr. Butterworth, and Mr. Allan the lawyer, two of the most influential London Methodists, were placed on this Committee, with other laymen. In this Committee of Privileges, and in the Missionary Committee, laymen gradually took their share in the counsels of the Connexion. They were next introduced to the Home Missionary and Chapel Committees. Out of the Annual Home Missionary gathering sprang a system of Committees of Review, into which the principle of direct representation was introduced in 1861. Sagacious men recognized that this was an important step in the right direction, likely to prevent the Connexional disputes and eruptions from which Methodism had suffered in the past.

The Conference of 1878 witnessed the introduction of laymen into the chief assembly of Methodism. After prolonged deliberation a Representative Session of 240 ministers and 240 laymen had been constituted in 1877, and to them all business not affecting ministerial character or pastoral work is committed. At first the Representative Session met in the third week after the Pastoral Session had closed, but this arrangement proved inconvenient, and in 1891 it began to meet in the second week. Besides the Circuit Stewards who attend the District Meeting for the transaction of business, not purely pastoral, each circuit elects representative lay members to the Synod. One is chosen where the circuit has only one minister, and two where there are three ministers or upwards. This regulation came into force in 1893. The term District Synod was adopted in 1892.

Educational Work.— In the year 1843, a bill for the better education of children in factory districts was brought into the House of Commons, which virtually handed over these children to the Established Church. After the bill was withdrawn, the

Conference of 1843 passed a resolution affirming that "the Wesleyan Connexion is now imperatively called upon, not only efficiently to maintain its own Educational operations, but also greatly to enlarge them, by the formation of week-day schools in every Circuit wherever it is practicable." The following October an influential Committee met in London. It resolved that if possible, seven hundred schools should be established during the next seven years, and that an Education Fund should be created which should amount, if possible, to £5,000 a year. The Centenary Fund had already appropriated £5,000 for Wesleyan Day Schools. In 1847, the Government proposed to make liberal grants towards training colleges for teachers, as well as for elementary schools. Methodism took its part in this national work, and built its college at Westminster. The Rev. John Scott, who had been Chairman of the Education Committee, became the first Principal of this college, and his influence and authority proved invaluable during the formative years that followed. After his death in 1868, Dr. Rigg was appointed his successor. Up till 1871 both day-school masters, and mistresses, were trained at Westminster, but in that year a new college for female teachers was opened at Battersea. In these colleges Christian teachers have been trained for service, not only in Wesleyan Schools, but in the Board Schools of the country. No training colleges are more efficient, and the Biblical and Theological lectures given by the Principal are a very important part of the curriculum. Westminster provides for 120, and Southlands for 110 students. There are now 786 Wesleyan Day Schools, with 163,000 scholars.

Methodism has also taken its share in higher education. Wesley College, Sheffield, led the way in 1837; Taunton College followed a little later. The Leys School was founded at Cambridge under Dr. Moulton as Head Master in 1874. A great impetus was given to Methodist middle-class Schools by the Thanksgiving Fund. There are now efficient Methodist Schools at Truro, Jersey, Bury St. Edmunds, Congleton, Canterbury, Folkestone, Trowbridge, Penzance, Camborne, and Queenswood, Clapham. Woodhouse Grove, which was opened for Ministers' sons in 1812, is now a middle-class School.

The Thanksgiving Fund.—It was felt that an event so memorable as the introduction of lay representatives to the Conference ought to find some permanent memorial. The Thanksgiving Fund was therefore formed, and under the guidance of Dr. Rigg, the President of the Conference in 1878, it soon became a magnificent success. The meetings held on its behalf in all parts of the Connexion were an inspiration. £297,500 was raised, which was thus distributed :

Foreign Missions	£63,869	Middle Class Schools	£10,000
Extension of Methodism	45,000	Necessitous Local Preachers	8,000
Theological Institution	38,817	Sunday School Union	6,000
Schools Fund	37,878	Methodism in Scotland	4,907
Handsworth College	25,000	Invalid Ministers' Rest Fund	4,000
Children's Home and Princess Alice Orphanage	24,168	Welsh Chapels	3,984
		London German Chapel	2,002
Home Missions	21,000	Oxford New Chapel	2,000
Education Fund	14,000	Temperance Committee	2,000

Great Town Missions.—Up to the year 1885 the state of some of the town chapels had been regarded as almost hopeless. Members had removed to the suburbs, and venerable sanctuaries were almost deserted. The appointment of the Rev. S. F. Collier to Oldham Street, and the Rev. Edward Smith to the London Mission, soon created new hope, and ever since then the tide of enthusiasm and of success has been rising. In Manchester 10,000 to 12,000 people attend the mission services every Sunday night. There are also 2,500 Sunday scholars, and 1,200 men and women meeting in Bible Classes. In London, St. James' Hall is crowded, and a thousand people have been turned away from Mr. Hughes' evening service. Clerkenwell is a wonderful artisan congregation; Southwark and Locksfields are filled. St. George's has become the centre of a great rescue work in the East End. Birmingham, Nottingham, Hull, Cardiff, Leicester, Coventry, Newcastle-on-Tyne, Sunderland, Leeds, Liverpool, Edinburgh, Glasgow, and many other towns have a similar record. Methodism has not only shown its power to gather crowds of people, but its mission workers have proved that by wise social measures it is possible to reach the most degraded, and win them for Christ.

Village Methodism.—The same spirit has borne fruit in village Methodism. East Anglia has witnessed a wonderful revival. Nineteen chapels which had been closed, have been re-opened, and the whole district is now being worked in a new spirit. In Devon and Dorset, and in Wiltshire our Village Missions have taken firm root, and are growing stronger every day. The South Wales Mission is gaining strength. Sisters of the people and Deaconesses are taking a foremost place in the modern Home Mission movement. By nursing the sick and visiting the homes of the poor they have done much to win the goodwill of the masses, and lay a firm basis for the Evangelistic successes which are reported from all quarters.

Work among Children.—Dr. Stephenson's work for destitute and orphan children is one of the chief glories of modern Methodism. It began quietly in Lambeth in 1869, and two years later was transferred to Bethnal Green, where it still has its head quarters. It has a branch at Edgworth, near

Bolton, a reformatory school near Gravesend, an orphanage at Birmingham, a happy little settlement at Ramsey, in the Isle of Man, and an emigration depôt in Canada. The number of boys and girls in residence is about a thousand, the income exceeds £24,000. Sunday schools send more than £3,000 a year to the treasury, and the Home is strong in the affection of both young and old. Its operations are by no means limited to Wesleyan children. It considers every appeal, and does its utmost, so far as funds will allow, to help every waif and every orphan as well as every juvenile offender.

The Allan Library.—In 1884, Mr. T. R. Allan, son of the Wesleyan lawyer, who was one of the first members of the Committee of Privileges, gave to Methodism, through Dr. Rigg, the valuable library which he had been collecting for many years. It was established in its present spacious quarters at the Book Room in 1891, and was opened on March 4th. It is now open to preachers and people on payment of a small subscription, and arrangements have been made to send the books out to members in all parts of the country. It is full of literary curiosities. Few libraries are so rich in Biblical treasures, editions of the Fathers, and Reformation literature. It is beginning to attract Methodist books from all quarters, and a considerable infusion of modern works has been added. Its value as a great Methodist reference library will become more manifest as years pass by.

Centenary of Wesley's Death.—The Centenary of Wesley's death was kept with great solemnity in 1891. A memorable series of services thronged City Road Chapel for a whole week, and meetings were held throughout Methodism, in which the spirit of thanksgiving and hope seemed to sway all hearts. Wesley's work in all its breadth and significance, was recognised as it had never been recognised before. Dean Farrar, then Canon of Westminster, expressed the feeling of all Christian thinkers, when he said at City Road, " I say that even now I do not think we have done sufficient honour to the work which Wesley did. Consider the fact that he gave an impulse to all missionary exertion—the British and Foreign Bible Society, the Religious Tract Society, the London Missionary Society. Even the Church Missionary Society owes much to his initiative. The work of Education and the work of Ragged Schools—the work of Robert Raikes the Gloucester printer, and John Pounds the Portsmouth cobbler—were partly anticipated when the sainted Silas Told taught at the Foundery. Wesley was the first to encourage the cheap press, with all its stupendous results; he was the first to make common in England the spread of religious education; he was a pioneer of funeral reform. Besides all these things, he was the inaugurator of prison reform, for he visited prisons and sought to improve them long before John Howard made that his special work ; and the very last letter he ever wrote was a letter written to Wilberforce to spur him on and encourage him in his brilliant advocacy of Emancipation for the Slaves. We may therefore feelingly endorse the estimate of one who said that almost everything in the religious history of modern days was foreshadowed by John Wesley. Wesley was the first man who revived the spirit of religion among the masses of the people, and who roused the slumbering Church. His was the voice that first offered the great masses of the people hope for the despairing, and welcome to the outcast ; and his work is continued under changed forms, not only in the founding of the great Wesleyan community, but also in the Evangelical movement in the Church of England itself; and even at this moment in the enthusiasm for humanity which is shown by the poor, humble, and despised Salvationists." In connexion with the Centenary a statue of John Wesley was placed in front of City Road Chapel, which was beautified and made more worthy of its position as the Cathedral of Methodism. Methodist Churches and people all over the world joyfully contributed funds for a work that was dear alike to all.

Funds.—The annual income of all Methodist funds including the amount raised for the support of the ministry, probably exceeds £1,500,000. During the thirty years preceding the centenary of Wesley's death, more than £8,000,000 was expended on Connexional property—chapels, houses and schools. The total debt remaining was not more than £800,000 equal to one year's income from the trust property of the Connexion. The erection of the Central Hall with the offices of the Chapel Committee in Manchester, forms one of the land-marks of the Forward Movement. Methodist Sunday Schools now number 7,139, with 965,201 scholars and 131,145 teachers. The Sunday School Union, at Ludgate Circus, is a prosperous business concern, and the visits of the Sunday School Secretary to all parts of the country are a great means of stimulating and guiding the workers. The Extension Fund, which was founded to promote the building of a thousand chapels, has already promised grants and loans amounting to £122,999, to 1796 chapel schemes. The Metropolitan Chapel Building Fund founded in 1862 has given £210,000 in grants and loans to help in the erection of about 100 new chapels. This Fund has transformed London Methodism. Before it was established, there were only three Methodist chapels of importance south of the Thames, now there are 39 ; north of City Road, the four have grown to 37 ; west of Manchester Square there was one, now

there are 26 ; east of Spitalfields there were three, now there
are 15. The names of Sir Francis Lycett and Sir William
M‘Arthur will always be associated with these funds, of which
they were princely supporters.

Statistics. –The progress of Methodism in the twenty-five
years after Wesley's death showed how groundless were the
fears of preachers and people.

MEMBERS.

	Great Britain.	Missions.	United States.
1790	71,668	5,300	43,265
1815	211,063	19,885	211,129
Increase	139,395	14,585	167,864

MINISTERS.

	Great Britain.	Missions.	United States.
1790	294	19	198
1815	868	74	687
Increase	564	55	489

There are now about ten thousand Wesleyan chapels and
other preaching places with accommodation for more than two
million hearers. There are nearly 19,000 Methodist lay
preachers in England, Scotland and Wales.

General Statistics of Methodism.

	MINISTERS AND PROBATIONERS.	MEMBERS (incl. those on trial.)
WESLEYAN METHODISTS—		
Great Britain	2,137	466,771
Ireland	230	27,576
Foreign Missions	378	52,068
French Conference	42	1,942
South African Conference	200	62,812
West Indian Conferences	111	50,365
Australasian Conferences	630	94,407
METHODIST NEW CONNEXION—		
England	187	33,914
Ireland	10	1,014
Missions	8	2,029
BIBLE CHRISTIANS—		
England	166	26,981
Australia, China, etc.	128	7,355
PRIMITIVE METHODISTS—		
England, etc.	1,118	196,324
UNITED METHODIST FREE CHURCHES—		
Home Districts	356	75,479
Foreign Districts	79	13,974
WESLEYAN REFORM UNION	17	7,992
INDEPENDENT METHODIST AND FREE GOSPEL CHURCHES	349	7,534

UNITED STATES—

Methodist Episcopal	15,539	2,350,726
Union American Meth. Episc.	115	7,031
African Methodist Episcopal	4,252	497,350
African Union Meth. Prot.	42	3,500
African Meth. Episc. Zion	2,372	394,562
Methodist Protestant	1,500	162,789
Wesleyan Methodist	600	16,492
Methodist Episcopal (South)	5,487	1,333,210
Congregational Methodist	150	8,765
Congregational Meth. (coloured)	5	319
New Congregational Methodist	20	1,059
Zion Union Apostolic	30	2,346
Coloured Methodist Episcopal	1,224	128,817
Primitive Methodist	65	5,005
Free Methodist	863	26,140
Independent Methodist	8	2,569
Evangelist Missionary	47	951

CANADA—

Methodist Church in Canada	2,064	267,740
Totals	40,529	6,337,908

N.B.—These statistics are the latest procurable. The membership of Junior Society Classes is not reckoned.

Testimonies.—Long before Wesley's death, he had outlived reproach, and was universally recognised as one of the noblest men, and most influential workers that England has produced. In 1876, Dean Stanley opened the doors of Westminster Abbey to the two brothers, whose tablet has become a kind of shrine for Methodist visitors from all corners of the earth. At the Wesleyan Centenary, Dr. Dale showed that Nonconformity owes no small debt to Methodism, for religious life and zeal caught from its altars. " William Jay, of Bath, discovered the glory and grace of the Christian redemption at a Methodist service. My colleague and predecessor, John Angell James, did not attribute his religious decision to Methodist preaching ; but he says in his Autobiography, that when a boy at Blandford, the only religious fire in the town was among the Methodists ; he was taken by his mother to the Methodist meetings on Sunday nights, and there was a touch of Methodism in him to the very last. He always smelled of that fire. Thomas Raffles, of Liverpool, in his early life, was a member of the Wesleyan Society. John Leifchild, of Craven, was originally one of your local preachers. The great revival which originated Methodism, restored life, vigour, courage, fervour to the Congregational Churches of England?" Dr. Stoughton's father and mother, grandfather and grandmother were all Methodists.

Dr. Parker gained experience as a Methodist local preacher. Mr. Spurgeon was led to Christ by a Primitive Methodist lay preacher. Dan Taylor, the Yorkshire miner, who founded the New Connexion of General Baptists in 1770, was converted under Wesley's preaching. Nor does the Church of England owe less to Methodism. Mr. J. R. Green says, " The Methodists themselves were the least result of the Methodist Revival. Its action upon the Church broke the lethargy of the clergy." Mr. Lecky bears this testimony to the movement. " The creation of a large, powerful, and active sect, extending over both hemispheres, and numbering many millions of souls, was but one of its consequences. It also exercised a profound and lasting influence upon the spirit of the Established Church, and upon the amount and distribution of the moral forces of the nation, and even upon the course of its political history."

Position of Methodism.—Methodism is now the largest Protestant Church in the world, with something like twenty-five million adherents and Sunday scholars in all parts of the globe. If John Wesley were with us, he would preach from the text which he chose for his review of Methodist history on laying the foundation stone of City Road Chapel : " According-ing to this time, it shall be said, what hath God wrought ! " The Connexion has been true to its Founder's boast : " The Methodists are the friends of all, the enemies of none." It has steadily cultivated sympathy with all Christian people, and with all true work for Christ. It has recognized that some of its own best fruit has been gained through that quickening of religious life and zeal, which it has brought about outside its own borders. From the beginning it has sought to keep aloof from party politics, and quietly to fulfil its own mission of spreading Scriptural holiness throughout the land. Methodism is now one of the greatest forces of the world, and if its preachers and people are loyal to Wesley's principles—personal religion and personal service—there is a glorious future for our Church. No other Church gives its laity such influence in its councils, or opens to them such doors of usefulness. There is ample room for development and adaptation to the various needs of the time. In that respect Methodism is true to its Founder's spirit, for his whole system was a series of adaptations to the religious wants of his age. Unceasing prayer and unceasing work will make Methodism bear still greater fruit for God, and for the world.

Dr. Parker gained experience as a Methodist local preacher. Mr. Spurgeon was led to Christ by a Primitive Methodist lay preacher. Dan Taylor, the Yorkshire miner, who founded the New Connexion of General Baptists in 1770, was converted under Wesley's preaching. Nor does the Church of England owe less to Methodism. Mr. J. R. Green says, "The Methodists themselves were the least result of the Methodist Revival. Its action upon the Church broke the lethargy of the clergy." Mr. Lecky bears this testimony to the movement. "The creation of a large, powerful, and active sect, extending over both hemispheres, and numbering many millions of souls, was but one of its consequences. It also exercised a profound and lasting influence upon the spirit of the Established Church, and upon the amount and distribution of the moral forces of the nation, and even upon the course of its political history."

Position of Methodism.—Methodism is now the largest Protestant Church in the world, with something like twenty-five million adherents and Sunday scholars in all parts of the globe. If John Wesley were with us, he would preach from the text which he chose for his review of Methodist history on laying the foundation stone of City Road Chapel: " According to this time, it shall be said, what hath God wrought ! " The Connexion has been true to its Founder's boast : " The Methodists are the friends of all, the enemies of none." It has steadily cultivated sympathy with all Christian people, and with all true work for Christ. It has recognized that some of its own best fruit has been gained through that quickening of religious life and zeal, which it has brought about outside its own borders. From the beginning it has sought to keep aloof from party politics, and quietly to fulfil its own mission of spreading Scriptural holiness throughout the land. Methodism is now one of the greatest forces of the world, and if its preachers and people are loyal to Wesley's principles—personal religion and personal service—there is a glorious future for our Church. No other Church gives its laity such influence in its councils, or opens to them such doors of usefulness. There is ample room for development and adaptation to the various needs of the time. In that respect Methodism is true to its Founder's spirit, for his whole system was a series of adaptations to the religious wants of his age. Unceasing prayer and unceasing work will make Methodism bear still greater fruit for God, and for the world.

www.ingramcontent.com/pod-product-compliance
Lightning Source LLC
Chambersburg PA
CBHW022022080426
42733CB00007B/689